Researching the Law

How to use your Connected Casebook

Step 1: Go to **www.CasebookConnect.com** and redeem your access code to get started.

Access Code:

Step 2: Go to your **BOOKSHELF** and select your Connected Casebook to start reading, highlighting, and taking notes in the margins of your e-book.

Step 3: Select the **STUDY** tab in your toolbar to access a variety of practice materials designed to help you master the course material. These materials may include explanations, videos, multiple-choice questions, flashcards, short answer, essays, and issue spotting.

Step 4: Select the **OUTLINE** tab in your toolbar to access chapter outlines that automatically incorporate your highlights and annotations from the e-book. Use the My Notes area for copying, pasting, and editing your book notes or creating new notes.

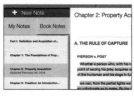

Step 5: If your professor has enrolled your class, you can select the **CLASS INSIGHTS** tab and compare your own study center results against the average of your classmates.

Is this a used casebook? Access code already scratched off?

You can purchase the Digital Version and still access all of the powerful tools listed above. Please visit CasebookConnect.com and select Catalog to learn more.

ASPEN COURSEBOOK SERIES

Researching the Law

Finding What You Need When You Need It

Third Edition

AMY E. SLOAN
Professor of Law
University of Baltimore School of Law

Wolters Kluwer

Published by Wolters Kluwer in New York.

Wolters Kluwer Legal & Regulatory U.S. serves customers worldwide with CCH, Aspen Publishers, and Kluwer Law International products. (www.WKLegaledu.com)

Cover image: akebonostock/stock.adobe.com

To contact Customer Service, e-mail customer.service@wolterskluwer.com, call 1-800-234-1660, fax 1-800-901-9075, or mail correspondence to:

Wolters Kluwer
Attn: Order Department
PO Box 990
Frederick, MD 21705

Printed in the United States of America.

1 2 3 4 5 6 7 8 9 0

ISBN 978-1-5438-1336-4

Library of Congress Cataloging-in-Publication Data

Names: Sloan, Amy E., 1964- author.
Title: Researching the law: finding what you need when you need it / Amy
    E. Sloan, Professor of Law, University of Baltimore School of Law.
Description: Third edition. | New York CIty: Wolters Kluwer, [2020] |
    Series: Aspen coursebook series | Includes index. | Summary: "Textbook
    for a first-year law school legal research course that offers a concise,
    accessible approach to teaching legal research" — Provided by publisher.
Identifiers: LCCN 2019056764 (print) | LCCN 2019056765 (ebook) | ISBN
    9781543813364 (paperback) | ISBN 9781543820980 (ebook)
Subjects: LCSH: Legal research — United States.
Classification: LCC KF240.S586 2020 (print) | LCC KF240 (ebook) | DDC
    340.072/073 — dc23
LC record available at https://lccn.loc.gov/2019056764
LC ebook record available at https://lccn.loc.gov/2019056765

About Wolters Kluwer Legal & Regulatory U.S.

Wolters Kluwer Legal & Regulatory U.S. delivers expert content and solutions in the areas of law, corporate compliance, health compliance, reimbursement, and legal education. Its practical solutions help customers successfully navigate the demands of a changing environment to drive their daily activities, enhance decision quality and inspire confident outcomes.

Serving customers worldwide, its legal and regulatory portfolio includes products under the Aspen Publishers, CCH Incorporated, Kluwer Law International, ftwilliam.com and MediRegs names. They are regarded as exceptional and trusted resources for general legal and practice-specific knowledge, compliance and risk management, dynamic workflow solutions, and expert commentary.

Summary of Contents

Contents ▼

Preface

Legal research, like every other aspect of legal practice, is changing rapidly in the face of new technologies. Research instruction used to focus on how to find useful information starting from nothing. Now, we are awash in information. The challenge has become one of narrowing large quantities of information to the subset of information necessary to solve a legal problem.

This book explains research from the standpoint of managing large quantities of information using pre- and post-search filtering processes. This third edition contains updated information to keep your research instruction current:

- Coverage of Westlaw, Lexis, and Bloomberg Law has been updated to reflect these services' latest functionality.
- The material on the weight of court opinions has been redesigned to address jurisdiction before level of court.
- The discussion of techniques for drafting effective word searches has been expanded and includes sample searches.
- New resources for evaluating and updating case research, such as visual mapping technologies and document analysis tools, are included.
- Material on case research with print digests has been moved to the end of the chapter after online search techniques.
- The description of statutory annotations has been revised to explain specifically where to find annotations in online sources.
- The Teacher's Manual and accompanying PowerPoint slides (available to faculty online from Wolters Kluwer) include updated instructional materials that can be used in class for a workshop approach to instruction.

Although the text has been updated, the structure and philosophy remain unchanged. Part I of the text addresses research process. It explains how a researcher defines a research question. It then shows how to pre-filter content before beginning a search based on the goals of the research and any knowledge the researcher already possesses about the research question. The text next explains techniques for conducting research and criteria for post-search filtering of search results to target the most useful information.

Part II of the text contains information about individual sources of authority. This part explains the most essential information about each source. It also describes sources and search strategies unique to each form of authority. Part III contains research flowcharts students can use to plan their research strategy for different types of research projects.

This book contains all the information a student needs to learn the fundamental principles of legal research. Because it is a concise book, however, it can also be used to complement other texts or instructional materials on legal research and writing.

Research is fundamentally a problem-solving process. My goal with this book is to provide a problem-solving framework that students can use to learn about research. Beyond that, I hope to convey a process that students can adapt to their future needs as they become proficient in research and as new technologies continue to change the way we do legal research.

Amy E. Sloan
January 2020

Acknowledgments ▼

I am indebted to many people for their help with this book. Many wonderful people at Wolters Kluwer worked on this book. I am indebted to Kathy Langone, Tom Daughhetee, and others at The Froebe Group without whom this book could not have been produced. Adeen Postar (former director of the University of Baltimore Law Library) and Harvey Morrell (current acting director) gave me valuable feedback. Caylee Henderson provided invaluable research assistance.

The third edition of this text builds on the first two editions. I continue to be grateful to Linda Berger, Joanne Colvin, Todd Culliton, Kirsten Davis, Bethany Henneman, Anne Kringel, Jennifer Lear, Andrea Murphy, Katrina Smith, and Michael Smith for their assistance with earlier editions.

And, as always, I thank my family for their love and support — Peggy, Andrew, and Jack, I couldn't accomplish anything without the three of you.

Researching
the Law

Research Process

Introduction to Legal Research

A. INTRODUCTION ▼

Information used to be a scarce resource. Legal information in particular was hard to find because it required access to a law library and specialized knowledge about how to locate information in law books. A generation ago, few people other than lawyers had both access and specialized knowledge. Lawyers had access and knowledge, but they had to dig through many different kinds of books to find the information they needed to advise their clients.

The Internet changed this, as it has changed virtually every other aspect of society. Information is no longer scarce. Huge amounts of it are at our fingertips. Consequently, anyone can access legal information, and search engines provide an easy way to locate that information. Lawyers do not struggle so much with uncovering scarce nuggets of useful information as with sorting through vast quantities of data to isolate the pieces that are relevant to their clients.

Despite these changes, the thought process necessary for effective legal research has not changed. The criteria lawyers used to drive the search process when legal information was only available in the books in a law library are the same criteria that help them sift the information they locate in other ways today. The goals of this book are to describe the research thought process, explain the criteria that drive that process, and illustrate how to use that process effectively. By mastering this process, you will learn to be an effective legal researcher.

B. THE RESEARCH THOUGHT PROCESS ▼

When you think about doing research, how do you envision the task? Do you think about finding *the* answer to *a* question? Research can involve finding a specific piece of information, or it can be a more complex process. Regardless of its complexity, however, research in any form is a systematic inquiry into a subject. The way you research is a function of why you need the information, what you know about the subject before you begin to search, and how well you are able to assess the usefulness of what you find.

The kinds of research people do in their daily lives are typically intended to give them information to make decisions. You watch a stock price to decide whether to buy, hold, or sell a security. You find a weather report to decide what to wear today or how to pack for an upcoming trip. The same is true of legal research. Lawyers conduct legal research to find information they use to help clients make decisions and solve problems. Virtually all kinds of research, including legal research, involve the following five steps:

- Determine what information you need.
- Choose a method of locating the information.
- Search for the information.
- Assess the information you find.
- Repeat the process until you have the information you need to make a decision.

The complexity of each of these steps and the number of times you repeat the process will vary according to your needs, as the following three examples illustrate.

Example 1: Answering a specific question with a defined answer. Assume you are cooking spinach manicotti with a recipe that lists ingredients in metric measures and calls for 60 milliliters of olive oil. You need to convert milliliters to U.S. measures. This is a specific question that you know has a definite answer. If you have a cookbook, it might include a conversion table you can use. If not, most people would Google the question. The search results would include links to a number of websites with the answer, and the answer would likely appear in the summary under each link. Because multiple sites all give the same answer, you would be confident that 60 milliliters is roughly 1/4 cup and would have no need to repeat the search.

Example 2: Answering a specific question without a defined answer.
Now step back and assume you want to cook spinach manicotti and need to find a recipe. This is similar to searching for a defined piece of information in that you have a specific question you seek to answer. It is a different type of research task, however, because there is no single recipe for spinach manicotti. You could find recipes in a variety of ways:

- Googling **"spinach manicotti"** and reviewing the cooking websites in the search results;
- going directly to a cooking website;
- calling a friend or family member whom you know has cooked the dish before;
- consulting a print cookbook.

Notice that all of the choices except Google require you to know a potential source of information before you begin the search (a website, person, or cookbook). Google allows you to search without thinking much about what you want to find, but it also requires you to sort through more irrelevant content when you review the results as compared with the other choices.

Additionally, consider how you would gather and evaluate recipes. You would probably use two or three of the sources listed above and compare the recipes before making a choice. The recipes you locate would likely be similar but not identical. You would have to choose which one to follow or how to combine aspects of different recipes. The recipe from a gourmet website might sound delicious but be too complicated to prepare. The quick and easy version could be similar to a recipe you got from a friend who is a good cook. Your personal taste, the ingredients you have on hand, and other criteria could also affect your choice.

Example 3: Researching an undefined inquiry.
Now assume that you are bored with what you have been cooking and are looking for a recipe for something new. This is different from researching a specific question because you do not have a specific idea of what you are looking for.

The sources you would use could be the same as the ones you would use for finding a specific recipe:

- Googling **"recipes"** and reviewing the cooking websites in the search results;
- going directly to a cooking website;
- calling a friend or family member for ideas;
- consulting a print cookbook.

Although you could use the same sources, the way you would use them would be different. You might review the index or table of contents of the cookbook, browse the recipe categories on the cooking website, or scan the results of the Google search. You would ask your friend or family member for a list of recommendations, not for a specific recipe. Of course, searching for "recipes" is very broad. If you could, you would want to try to focus your inquiry even before you begin to search based on criteria you select (Italian, vegetarian, gourmet, quick and easy).

Once you have conducted some research, you would evaluate the results and perhaps repeat the search process. As you search, you would narrow the choices according to what appeals to your personal taste, the ingredients you have on hand, the complexity of the recipe, the reputation of the recipe's source, or other factors. You might end up making spinach manicotti, but you would not have known that when you started the research process.

These examples might not seem like they have anything to do with legal research, but they illustrate several principles that apply to legal research: The goal of the research affects the research process. Sometimes you need to find *the* answer to a specific question. In the first example above, the conversion of 60 milli*liters* to U.S. measures is not the same as the conversion of 60 milli*grams*, and it would be important to find the right answer for the recipe to work. Similarly, if a specific legal rule determines the outcome of a client's situation, you must locate that rule to advise your client appropriately.

Although research sometimes involves finding *the* answer to *a* question, that is not always the case. Sometimes a legal rule is clear, but whether it should apply in a particular circumstance may be more ambiguous. Sometimes different aspects of a legal principle are stated in multiple sources that have to be read together for a complete picture of the law. Thus, research can involve locating a body of relevant information and then synthesizing that information to make a decision.

Moreover, what you know before you begin affects how you do research because the more you know, the easier it is to target relevant information and assess the usefulness of your research results. The less you know, the harder it is to sort through the research results to identify the body of relevant information.

Finally, research is usually a recursive process. Unless you are looking for an identifiable piece of information, you will probably search and evaluate repeatedly, gradually filtering your research results until you isolate the most useful information.

C. A PROCESS FOR LEGAL RESEARCH   ▼

The process of legal research is closer to a dance with an overlapping pattern of steps than a regimented march. Research instruction usually proceeds through a series of set steps, however, which can make the process seem more linear (and inflexible) than it really is. Following a linear process can be a good way to learn something new. You must begin and end your research somewhere. Following a defined path as you learn about research both helps you understand what you need to do and guides you as you gain confidence in your ability. But the real life process of doing research rarely proceeds in such a linear fashion. What you know before you start and what you learn as you research will affect the nature and order of the steps you follow.

Although research process must be flexible, it is not random, and finding the information you need is not a matter of chance. Researching is a skill you can learn, just as writing is a skill you can learn. By mastering an organized approach to research, you will be able to find the information you need quickly and efficiently. This book illustrates a research process you can follow as a beginning researcher and later customize to your needs as you gain experience.

As you learn about legal research, you may find it helpful to structure your thoughts around the following questions:

▼ **What question(s) do I need to answer?**
At the start of your research, you need to articulate a research question so you will know what you are looking for. If the question is broad, you might need to break it down into a series of more defined subsidiary questions.

▼ **How can I use the information I already have to focus my research?**
The more you can focus your search before you begin, the easier it will be to isolate the information that is responsive to your research question. Effective pre-search filtering requires you to be familiar with the sources of legal information and their organization. You can use this information to focus both where and how you look for relevant information.

▼ **What criteria should I use to evaluate what I find?**
As you conduct research, you need to evaluate the search results. The criteria you use to evaluate your search results will be a function of the authoritative weight of different sources of law and their relevance to the question you seek to answer.

▼ **How can I use what I find to locate more or better information?**
Often, you will need to use the information from your initial search results to refine your research question(s), change the sources or search techniques you use, and assess the criteria for focusing your search results. Then you will likely need to repeat the process multiple times until you have isolated the subset of legal information necessary to answer your research question.

The American Legal System

What is the law? "Law" usually means the rules created by government entities that govern conduct in society. These rules may require or prohibit certain types of conduct. They may establish standards for resolving disputes or accomplishing tasks. Lawyers research legal rules to help clients make decisions and solve problems in ways that conform to the law's requirements.

To understand how to identify and locate the law relevant to a client's situation, you need to understand the sources of and relationships among different types of legal rules in the American legal system. You also need to understand how legal information is organized.

A. SOURCES OF LAW ▼

Four main sources of law exist at both state and federal levels:

- constitutions;
- statutes;
- court opinions (also called cases);
- administrative regulations.

A constitution establishes a system of government and defines the boundaries of authority granted to the government. The U.S. Constitution is the preeminent source of law in our legal system, and all other rules, whether adopted by a state or the federal government, must comply with the federal Constitution's requirements. Each state also has its own constitution. A state's constitution may grant greater rights than those secured by the federal Constitution. But because state law is subordinate to the federal Constitution, a state cannot provide lesser rights than those secured by the federal Constitution. All of a state's legal rules must comport with both the state and federal constitutions.

Since grade school, you have been taught that the U.S. Constitution created three branches of government: the legislative branch, which makes the laws; the judicial branch, which interprets the laws; and the executive branch, which enforces the laws. State governments are also divided into these three branches. Although this is elementary civics, this structure truly does define the way government authority is divided in our system of government.

The legislative branch of government creates statutes, which must be approved by the executive branch (the president, for federal statutes; the governor, for state statutes) to go into effect. The executive branch also makes rules. Administrative agencies, such as the federal Food and Drug Administration or a state's department of motor vehicles, are part of the executive branch. They execute the laws passed by the legislature and create their own regulations to carry out the mandates established by statute.

The judicial branch is the source of court opinions, which are also called cases. Courts interpret rules created by the legislative and executive branches of government. If a court determines that a rule does not meet constitutional requirements, it can invalidate the rule. Otherwise, however, the court must apply the rule to the case before it. Cases can also be an independent source of legal rules. Legal rules made by courts are called "common-law" rules. Although courts are empowered to make these rules, legislatures can adopt legislation that changes or abolishes a common-law rule, as long as the legislation is constitutional.

Figure 2.1 shows the relationships among the branches of government and the types of legal rules they create.

An example may be useful to illustrate the relationships among the rules created by the three branches of the federal government. As you know, the U.S. Constitution, through the First Amendment, guarantees the right to free expression. Congress could pass legislation requiring television stations to provide educational programming for children. The Federal Communications Commission (FCC) is the administrative agency within the executive branch that would be responsible for carrying out Congress's will. If the statute were not specific about what constitutes educational programming or how much educational programming must be provided, the FCC would have to create administrative regulations to execute the law. The regulations would provide the information not detailed in the statute, such as the definition of educational programming. A television station could challenge the statute and regulations by arguing to a court that prescribing the content of material the station must broadcast violates the First Amendment. The court would then have to interpret the statute and regulations to decide whether they comport with the Constitution.

Another example illustrates the relationship between courts and legislatures in the area of common-law rules. The rules of negligence have

▼ FIGURE 2.1   Branches of Government and Legal Rules

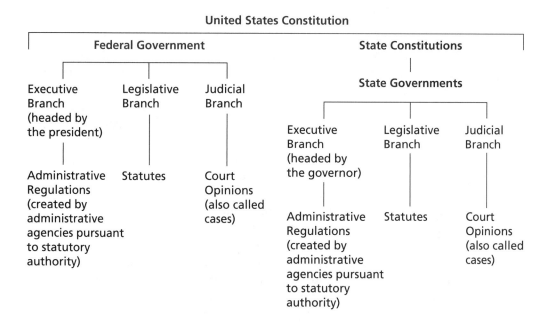

largely been created by the courts. Therefore, liability for negligence is usually determined by common-law rules. A state supreme court could decide that a plaintiff who sues a defendant for negligence cannot recover any damages if the plaintiff herself was negligent and contributed to her own injuries. This decision would create a common-law rule governing future cases of negligence within that state. The state legislature could step in and pass a statute that changes the rule. For example, the legislature could enact a statute providing that, when both the plaintiff and the defendant are negligent, juries are to determine the percentage of negligence attributable to each party and to apportion damages accordingly, instead of completely denying recovery to the plaintiff. Courts in that state would then be obligated to apply the rule from the statute, not the former common-law rule.

Although these examples are simplified, they demonstrate the basic roles of each of the branches of government in enunciating the legal rules governing conduct in society. They also demonstrate that researching a legal issue may require you to research several different types of legal authority. The answer to a research question may not be found exclusively in statutes or cases or administrative regulations. Often, these sources must be researched together to determine all of the rules applicable to a client's situation.

B. TYPES AND WEIGHT OF AUTHORITY ———————————▼

1. Types of Authority

One term used to describe the rules that govern conduct in society is "authority." Authority, however, is a broad term that can describe both legal rules that must be followed and other types of information that are not legal rules. To understand the weight, or authoritative value, an authority carries, you must learn to differentiate "primary" authority from "secondary" authority and "binding" authority from "nonbinding" authority.

Primary authority is a term used to describe a source of a rule of law. All of the sources of rules discussed so far in this chapter are primary authorities. Constitutional provisions, statutes, cases, and administrative regulations contain legal rules, and as a consequence, are primary authorities. Because "the law" consists of legal rules, primary authority is sometimes described as "the law."

Secondary authority, by contrast, refers to commentary on the law or analysis of the law, but not "the law" itself. An opinion from the U.S. Supreme Court is a primary authority, but an article written by a private party explaining and analyzing the opinion is a secondary authority. Secondary authorities are often quite useful in legal research because their analysis can help you understand complex legal issues and refer you to primary authorities. Nevertheless, a secondary authority is not "the law" and therefore is distinguished from a primary authority.

Binding and nonbinding authority are terms lawyers use to define the authoritative value of a source of law. Binding authority, which can also be called mandatory authority, refers to an authority that must be followed. In other words, a binding authority contains one or more rules that you must apply to determine the correct answer to your research question. Nonbinding authority refers to an authority that can be, but does not have to be, followed. Nonbinding authority is sometimes called persuasive authority. A nonbinding authority will not dictate the answer to your research question, but it may help you figure out the answer. Whether an authority is binding or nonbinding depends on several factors, as discussed in the next section.

2. Weight of Authority

The degree to which an authority controls the answer to a legal question is called the weight of the authority. Not all authorities have the same weight. The weight of an authority depends on its status as primary or secondary, as well as its status as binding or nonbinding.

An authority's status as a primary or secondary authority is fixed. An authority is either part of "the law," or it is not. Anything that does not fit into one of the categories of primary authority is secondary authority. Distinguishing primary authority from secondary authority is the first step in determining how much weight a particular authority has in the resolution of your research question. Then you can determine whether the authority is binding or nonbinding.

a. Secondary Authority: Always Nonbinding

Once you identify an authority as secondary, you can be certain that it will not control the outcome of the question you are researching because all secondary authorities are nonbinding. Nevertheless, some are more persuasive than others. Some are so respected that a court, while not technically bound by them, would need a good reason to depart from or reject their statements of legal rules. Others do not enjoy the same degree of respect, leaving a court free to ignore or reject such authorities if it is not persuaded to follow them. Further discussion of the persuasive value of various secondary authorities appears in Chapter 8. The important thing to remember for now is that secondary authorities are always categorized as persuasive or nonbinding.

b. Primary Authority: Sometimes Binding, Sometimes Nonbinding

Sometimes a primary authority is a binding, or mandatory, authority, and sometimes it is not. You must be able to evaluate the authority to determine whether it is binding on the question you are researching.

Jurisdiction is one factor affecting whether a primary authority is binding. A rule contained in a primary authority applies only within the jurisdiction where the authority is in force. For example, all laws in the United States must comport with the federal Constitution because it is a primary authority that is binding, or mandatory, in all U.S. jurisdictions. The New Jersey constitution is also a primary authority because it contains legal rules establishing the scope of state government authority, but it is a binding authority only in New Jersey. The New Jersey constitution's rules do not apply in Illinois or Michigan.

Determining the weight of a case is a little more complex. All cases are primary authorities. Whether a particular case is binding or nonbinding is a function not only of jurisdiction, but also level of court.

▼ Court system structures

In considering the weight of a case, it is important to remember that the federal government and each state constitute different jurisdictions because each has its own government. Consequently, the federal and state court systems are separate. Although the systems are separate, they are structured similarly. The federal and all state judicial systems have

▼ FIGURE 2.2   Structure of the Federal Court System and Most State
                Court Systems

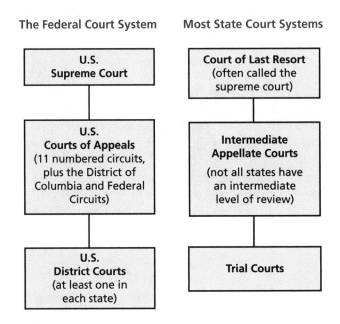

multiple levels of courts. Figure 2.2 illustrates the structures of federal
and state court systems.

Trial courts are at the bottom of the judicial hierarchy. In the federal
system, the United States District Courts are trial-level courts, and each
state has at least one federal district court.

Intermediate appellate courts hear appeals of trial court cases. Most
states, but not all, have intermediate appellate courts. In the federal system, the intermediate appellate courts are called United States Courts
of Appeals, and they are divided into 13 separate circuits: 11 numbered
circuits (First through Eleventh), the District of Columbia Circuit, and
the Federal Circuit.

The highest court or court of last resort within a jurisdiction is often
called the supreme court. It hears appeals of cases from the intermediate
appellate courts or directly from trial courts in states that do not have
intermediate appellate courts. In the federal system, of course, the court
of last resort is the United States Supreme Court.

To determine the weight of a case, you must evaluate both jurisdiction and level of court, as described below.

▼ Determining the weight of a case: jurisdiction
As with other forms of primary authority, cases are binding authorities
only within the court's jurisdiction. An opinion from the Texas Supreme

▼ FIGURE 2.3   Geographic Boundaries of the Federal Courts of Appeals

Federal Judicial Center 1999

Court is binding only for a court applying Texas law. A California court deciding a question of California law would consider the Texas opinion a nonbinding authority. If the California court had to decide a new issue not previously addressed by any binding California authorities (a "question of first impression"), it might choose to follow the Texas Supreme Court's opinion if it found the opinion persuasive.

On questions of federal law, opinions of the U.S. Supreme Court are binding on all other courts because it has nationwide jurisdiction. An opinion from a circuit court of appeals is binding on federal courts only within the circuit that issued the opinion. A decision of the U.S. Court of Appeals for the Eleventh Circuit, for example, would bind the federal courts located in the Eleventh Circuit but not the federal courts located in the Seventh Circuit. Figure 2.3 shows the geographic boundaries of the federal circuit courts of appeals.

Remember that the federal government and each state constitute different jurisdictions. On questions of state law, each state's courts get the last word, and on questions of federal law, the federal courts get the last word. This means that a federal opinion applying state law is not binding on the state courts, although it may be very persuasive.

Ordinarily, understanding how jurisdiction affects weight of authority is fairly intuitive. When a Massachusetts trial court resolves a case arising out of conduct that took place in Massachusetts, it will treat an opinion of the Massachusetts Supreme Judicial Court as a binding authority. Sometimes, however, a court has to resolve a case governed by the law of another jurisdiction. State courts sometimes decide cases governed by the law of another state or by federal law. Federal courts sometimes decide cases governed by state law. When that happens, the court deciding the case will treat the law of the controlling jurisdiction as binding.

For example, assume that the U.S. District Court for the Western District of Texas, a federal trial court, has to decide a case concerning breach of a contract to build a house in El Paso, Texas. Contract law is, for the most part, established by the states. To resolve this case, the federal court will apply the contract law of the state where the dispute arose, in this case, Texas. The Texas Supreme Court's cases on contract law are binding authorities for resolving the case because Texas law controls the resolution of the case.

Now assume that the same U.S. District Court has to decide a case concerning immigration law. Immigration law is established by the federal government. Therefore, the court will apply federal law to this case. The opinions of the U.S. Supreme Court and the U.S. Court of Appeals for the Fifth Circuit are binding authorities for this court in resolving the immigration case.

▼ Determining the weight of a case: level of court
The second step in determining the weight of a case is evaluating the level of the court that decided the case. To do this, recall the structure of most court systems: trial courts, intermediate appellate courts (if they exist within the jurisdiction), and court of last resort. You likely already know that decisions of higher courts typically carry more weight than those of lower courts.

Trial court opinions, including those from federal district courts, bind the parties to the cases but do not bind other trial courts considering similar cases, nor do they bind courts above them in the court structure. They are usually nonbinding, or persuasive, authority, even within the controlling jurisdiction.

The opinions of intermediate appellate courts bind lower courts, although you must know the jurisdiction's court structure to know precisely which courts are bound by which decisions. Generally, intermediate appellate cases are binding authorities for the trial courts directly subordinate to them in the jurisdiction's court structure. In jurisdictions with multiple appellate divisions, the opinions of one division may or may not bind trial courts in other divisions.

The weight of intermediate appellate cases on the intermediate appellate courts themselves varies. Again, in jurisdictions with multiple appellate divisions, the opinions of one division may or may not bind other divisions. In addition, in some circumstances, intermediate appellate courts can overrule their own prior opinions. Intermediate appellate cases are nonbinding authorities for the court of last resort.

The court of last resort may, but is not required to, follow the opinions of the courts below it. The opinions of the court of last resort, however, are binding authorities for both intermediate appellate courts and trial courts subordinate to it within the jurisdiction. The court of last resort is not bound by its own prior opinions but will be reluctant to change an earlier ruling without a compelling justification.

Figure 2.4 illustrates how a court's position within the judicial hierarchy affects the weight of its opinions.

c. Summary of Weight of Authority

This discussion provides an overview of some common principles governing the weight of authority. These principles are subject to exceptions and nuances not addressed here. Entire fields of study are devoted to resolving questions of jurisdiction, procedure, and conflicts regarding which legal rules apply to various types of disputes. As you begin learning about research, however, these general principles will help you determine the weight of the authorities you locate to resolve a research question. Figure 2.5 illustrates the relationships among the different types of authority.

▼ FIGURE 2.4   Level of Court and Weight of Authority

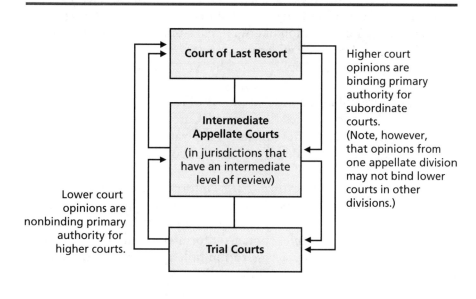

▼ **FIGURE 2.5**   Types of Authority

TYPE OF AUTHORITY	BINDING (MANDATORY)	NONBINDING (PERSUASIVE)
PRIMARY (legal rules)	Constitutional provisions, statutes, and regulations in force within a jurisdiction are binding authority for courts within the same jurisdiction. Decisions from higher courts within a jurisdiction are binding authority for lower courts within the same jurisdiction.	Decisions from courts within one jurisdiction are nonbinding authority for courts in other jurisdictions. Decisions from lower courts within a jurisdiction are nonbinding authority for higher courts within the same jurisdiction.
SECONDARY (anything that is not primary authority; usually commentary on the law)	Secondary authority is *not* binding authority.	Secondary authority is nonbinding authority.

C. HOW LEGAL INFORMATION IS ORGANIZED AND CITED ▼

Most, if not all, of the authorities you will learn to research are available from a variety of sources. They may be published in print, online, or in both formats. Online research services that provide access to legal publications include commercial databases that charge a fee for access and Internet sources freely available to anyone. Of course, you can obtain legal information from a general search engine like Google or a general source of information like Wikipedia, but lawyers tend to do the bulk of their legal research with more specialized research tools.

Most legal information is organized by type of authority and jurisdiction. In print, this means individual types of authority from individual jurisdictions are published in separate sets of books. Cases, for example, are published in books called "reporters." Cases from Florida will be in one set of reporters, and those from Pennsylvania will be in another set of reporters. The same holds true for print collections of statutes and other types of authority.

Online research tools devoted to legal information are organized similarly. Some are like print sets of reporters in that they provide access to one type of authority from one jurisdiction. The website for the Texas state legislature, for example, contains information only on Texas state legislation. Others provide access to multiple types of authority from many different jurisdictions. Although these services aggregate a wide range of authorities, they subdivide their contents, much like print sources, into individual databases organized by jurisdiction and type of authority. Many commercial and government sources provide online access to legal authorities. The Appendix at the end of this book lists the URLs for all of the resources discussed in this book, as well as others that you may find helpful.

Lexis and Westlaw are the best known online legal research services. Bloomberg Law is also becoming well known. All three are commercial databases that allow you to access all of the types of authorities discussed in this chapter. They charge subscribers for use of their services, although your law school undoubtedly subsidizes the cost of student research while you are in school. Other commercial and free research services you may encounter in law school include Fastcase, Casemaker, Findlaw, Casetext, and Cornell Law School's Legal Information Institute, among others. They provide access to many of the same types of authorities you can find in Lexis, Westlaw, and Bloomberg Law.

The organization of legal information by jurisdiction and type of authority affects the way individual legal authorities are identified. All legal authorities have citations assigned to them. The citation is the identifying information you can use to locate a document.

Citations were originally formulated so that researchers could find authorities in print. Although most authorities are now available online, they are still primarily identified by their print citations. In print research, the citation generally includes the name of the book in which the source is published, the volume of the book containing the specific item, and the page or section number where the item begins. For example, each case is identified by a citation containing the volume number of the reporter in which it is published, the name of the reporter, and the starting page of the opinion. If you had the citation for a case, you could locate it easily. Statutes, secondary sources, and other forms of authority also have citations you can use to retrieve specific documents.

When you present the results of your research in written form, you will need to include citations to the authorities you rely on. One place to find the rules for citing authority is *The Bluebook: A Uniform System of Citation.* Another source for rules on citation is the *ALWD Guide to Legal Citation* (formerly called the *ALWD Citation Manual*). Citations formatted with either set of rules look the same. You should use whichever citation manual your professor directs you to use. Additionally, some states have their own citation rules or style manuals that specify how different authorities are to be cited, and you may need to become familiar with these local rules to cite properly.

Defining a Research Question

Lawyers conduct legal research to obtain information to solve problems for clients. Thus, successful research requires you to ask the right questions to get the information you need. This chapter discusses how to define a research question and how to describe the concepts in the question in ways that are likely to lead to useful information.

A. WHAT QUESTION DO YOU NEED TO ANSWER? ▼

Lawyers use their accumulated knowledge, including both specialized knowledge gained in practice and foundational legal principles taught in law school, to figure out the questions they need to answer to solve a client's problem. Even as a beginning law student, you are being introduced to a body of information common to all lawyers that will help you figure out the questions a client's situation requires you to answer.

When you are first learning how to do research, your professor may define a research question for you (e.g., *What must a plaintiff show to establish the tort of battery in North Carolina?*). If you have been given a specific question to research, that is the question you should answer.

Often, however, part of your research task will be to define the question you need to answer. Sometimes you will need to answer a pure legal question like the one above about the tort of battery. More often, however, you will need to determine both which legal rules are relevant and how those rules apply to a particular factual scenario. A good research question asks a legal question in the context of the facts of the situation.

Here is a set of facts a client could present to you, followed by example research questions:

> Your client lives in North Carolina. He lives in a duplex with a front porch that extends across the entire front of the house. Your client's side of the porch is separated from his neighbor's side by a railing. The neighbor likes to smoke cigars on her own front porch, but the smoke travels to the client's front porch. The client told his neighbor that he finds the smell of the smoke intolerable. The neighbor had previously promised not to smoke on her front porch but regularly broke her promise, to the client's great consternation. One day, while the neighbor was smoking on her porch, the client berated her for breaking her promise. The neighbor, without saying a word, leaned over the railing separating the two porches, blew cigar smoke into the client's face, and sat back down on her own porch to finish the cigar. The client is upset about this interaction and wants to know whether he can recover damages from his neighbor.

If you were asked whether the client can prevail with a tort claim of battery against his neighbor, your question would be something like, *"Does a person commit the tort of battery by purposely blowing smoke in another person's face?"*

Because clients come to you with their problems and not defined legal questions, a more realistic scenario would be for the client to ask simply whether he has any remedy for his neighbor's conduct. This is a broader question that requires you to identify multiple research questions. If you can identify potentially relevant legal doctrines presented by your client's situation, you can use them to articulate research questions. You may already have learned enough about the law to identify three possible research questions presented in the scenario above:

> *Did the neighbor commit the tort of battery by purposely blowing smoke in the client's face?*
>
> *Did the neighbor trespass on the client's land by leaning over the porch railing?*
>
> *Did the neighbor breach a contract by breaking her promise?*

If you do not know the legal doctrines a situation presents, you can develop research questions using just the facts of the situation. Useful categories of facts include:

- the conduct of the parties;
- the mental states of the parties; and
- the injury suffered by the complaining party.

Claims and defenses often flow from these considerations; research questions organized around these types of facts can help you locate useful information.

Another approach is thinking in terms of people, places, and things. In the category of people, consider the parties in terms of their legal relationship. One party's legal obligation to another can turn on the nature of their relationship. You can generate useful research questions by focusing on the parties' legal status, such as neighboring landowners, landlord and tenant, parent and child, employer and employee, or doctor and patient.

In the category of places, consider where the conduct at issue occurred. The geographic location is important because it can determine jurisdiction. The type of location (e.g., a school or an office) is significant because it can affect which legal rules apply to the situation. In the category of things, both tangible objects like automobiles and intangible concepts like a vacation can help you develop a research question.

In the scenario described above, you could use the facts to develop research questions. Here are two examples:

The neighbor purposely blew smoke in the client's face knowing that the client was offended by the smoke. *Which legal theories apply when one person purposely offends another person by blowing smoke in his face?*

The neighbor promised not to smoke on her porch and then broke that promise. *Which legal theories apply when one person breaks a promise to another person?*

In these examples, notice that the facts are not expressed at the most concrete level. They are expressed at a level of abstraction intended to capture the type of situation they present, not the precise details of the client's circumstances. For example, focusing on cigar smoke would be too concrete. If the client has a legal remedy for being offended by smoke, it probably does not matter whether that smoke is from a cigar, cigarette, or pipe. Focusing on a broken promise not to smoke would be too concrete. If the client has a legal remedy for the broken promise, it probably does not matter whether the promise involved smoking or some other conduct.

On the other hand, the research question cannot be expressed so abstractly that it fails to capture the nature of the problem. For example, framing the question as, *"Under what circumstances does the law prohibit smoking?"* is too abstract to express the nature of the legal problem the situation presents. The art of defining the inquiry is to express it concretely enough to describe the nature of the problem you are trying to solve but also abstractly enough to lead you toward relevant information, even if that information is not addressed with precise specificity to the problem.

The more you know about the law and the facts at the start of your research, the easier it will be to define research questions. If you know little about the law, the facts, or both, you will probably have to return to this step several times as your research increases your understanding.

B. WHAT TERMS ARE LIKELY TO DESCRIBE WHAT YOU ARE LOOKING FOR? ▼

The next step in your research is generating search terms that describe the information you seek. You will use these terms in a search engine, index, or similar research tool to locate documents relevant to your research question.

The legal theories and facts in your research question will obviously be a good starting point. If you want to research the torts of battery and trespass to land, "battery" and "trespass" should be two of your search terms. Beyond this, however, developing a comprehensive list of search terms is a necessary step in the research process for two reasons: First, generating a list of search terms may cause you to change or add to your research question. Second, the research sources you consult may use different terms to describe relevant information. Developing a list of terms that could be used to describe the concepts in your research question will help ensure that you find the information you seek.

You have several options for categorizing the information in your research question to create an initial list of search terms. The categories you can use to develop a research question can also be used to create a comprehensive list of search terms:

- the legal theories at issue if you know them;
- the conduct and mental states of the parties;
- the injury suffered by the complaining party;
- the people involved in the situation, described by their legal status or relationship; and
- the places and things associated with the situation.

Once you have developed an initial set of search terms for your research question, the next task is to try to expand that list. The terms you originally generated may not be used in sources of relevant information. The relevant concepts may be expressed with synonyms or with language that is either more abstract or more concrete than your initial search terms. Therefore, once you have developed your initial search terms, you should try to increase both the breadth and the depth of the list.

Increasing the breadth of your list with synonyms and related terms is essential to your research strategy. This is especially true when you use

▼ FIGURE 3.1   Expanding the Breadth of Search Terms

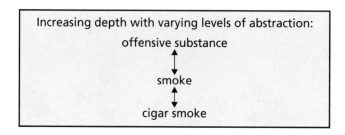

Increasing breadth with synonyms and related terms:

patio ◄──► porch ◄──► yard

▼ FIGURE 3.2   Increasing the Depth of Search Terms

Increasing depth with varying levels of abstraction:

offensive substance

▲
▼

smoke

▲
▼

cigar smoke

search engines that search literally for the precise terms you specify. In the research scenario described above, there are a number of synonyms and related terms for one of the facts in the scenario: porch. As Figure 3.1 illustrates, you might also search for terms such as patio or yard.

You are also more likely to find useful research material if you increase the depth of your list by varying the level of abstraction. The research scenario described above involves cigar smoke. As noted above, expressing this idea more abstractly as "smoke" might be useful. You could also express it even more abstractly as an "offensive substance." See Figure 3.2.

A dictionary is a useful tool for expanding your search terms. Many dictionaries list synonyms along with definitions. Additionally, although a thesaurus may suggest related terms, dictionary definitions can often help you vary the degree of abstraction at which you express the concepts in your research question. Look up the word "smoke" in a thesaurus and a dictionary to see the differences in the information they provide. A legal dictionary can also help you identify relevant legal theories.

C. SEARCH TERM CHART ───────────────▼

You can use Figure 3.3, the chart on the next page, to generate an initial list of search terms for a research question, as well as to expand the breadth and depth of the list. The chart is intended only as a guide; you may not be able to complete every block for every research question.

▶ FIGURE 3.3   Search Terms Chart

CATEGORIES OF INFORMATION	INITIAL SEARCH TERMS	INCREASED BREADTH (synonyms or related terms)	INCREASED DEPTH (varying degrees of abstraction)
Parties involved • Describe parties according to their relationships to each other (e.g., landlord and tenant)			
Places and things These can include the following: • Geographic location (e.g., North Carolina) • Type of location (e.g., school or office) • Tangible objects (e.g., automobiles) • Intangible concepts (e.g., vacation)			
Potential claims and defenses If these are not apparent, consider the following: • Parties' conduct (acts done and not done) • Parties' mental states • Injury suffered			
Relief sought by the complaining or injured party			
Additional categories			

Pre-Search Filtering

Once you have articulated a research question and generated a list of search terms, the next step is engaging in pre-search filtering to focus your research. Your ultimate goal in most research projects will be to locate binding primary authorities, if they exist, to resolve your research question. If binding primary authority is not available or does not directly answer your research question, nonbinding authorities (either primary or secondary) might help you analyze the issue. The search methods and tools you use to locate information will be driven, at least in part, by how much you can filter the information you need before you begin searching.

A. HOW PRE-SEARCH FILTERING AFFECTS RESEARCH ___▼

When you use a general search engine like Google, you type a query in the search box and retrieve results based on the content of the query. You do not have to limit the search according to any criteria other than the content of the information you seek. After you run the search, you must filter the search results by source or other criteria to identify useful information.

When you go to Wikipedia to locate information, you have selected a source before executing a search. You engaged in pre-search filtering by limiting the search to a source likely to give you the information you need.

You can easily experience the difference pre-search filtering makes for yourself. Search for the term *battery* (only *battery*, no other search terms) using both Google and Wikipedia, and locate a definition of the tort of battery in the search results. Look specifically for battery as a tort, not a crime. With the Google search, you must sort through advertisements for batteries and other information to find the definition. With the Wikipedia search, you still have some post-search filtering to do, but less than you do with the Google search because pre-filtering by source eliminated some irrelevant information before you executed the search.

▼ FIGURE 4.1   Pre- and Post-Search Filtering

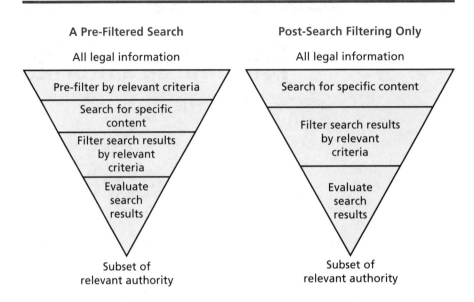

No matter how you conduct research, you will have to sift the information you find, as Figure 4.1 illustrates. There are no short cuts through this process. The more you can focus your search before you start your research, the less you will need to filter the results. The less pre-search filtering you do, the more sifting you will have to do after you obtain information.

The type of pre-search filtering you do depends on the nature of your research project and your ability to focus the search before you begin. To pre-filter by source, you have to think carefully about your research question to figure out which sources are most likely to contain relevant information. Although selecting a source can be challenging, choosing specific sources of information to research can make it easier to evaluate the results because they are confined to the particular type of information you selected. Indeed, a savvy researcher may know exactly what type of legal authority governs an issue — such as a state statute — and might not want to bother sifting through other types of information. Conversely, if you are not sure which source(s) of information to use, you could miss some relevant material altogether if you focus too narrowly on a particular source to the exclusion of others.

The research tools available to you will also affect your pre-search filtering. In some situations, you will have to pre-filter by source because the information in the available research tools will be organized by source into separate databases or books. Some online research services require you to select a database before you execute a search. Some websites only provide a certain type of information, so you have to know you need that type of information for the site to be useful. Print research also requires you to pre-filter by source. In print, each jurisdiction's cases are in different reporters, each jurisdiction's statutes are in different code books, and other forms of authority are published in separate sets of books.

With many online services (including Westlaw, Lexis, and Bloomberg Law) you can, but do not have to, pre-filter a search. These services allow you to search for content without any filters, just as you might with Google. They also allow you to pre-filter your search by selecting a specific jurisdiction and by following menu options to limit your search to a specific type of authority or legal topic.

If you skip pre-search filtering, you shift most of the analytical work involved in research to post-search filtering. Searching many sources simultaneously can be a good strategy because the search results can include sources you might not have considered using. On the other hand, this approach frequently retrieves a large amount of information that has to be sifted carefully. Retrieving hundreds or thousands of documents can feel overwhelming and can make post-search filtering difficult.

Forgoing pre-search filtering also limits the search techniques available to you. When you limit your search by source before you begin, you will often have a range of search options available, such as locating document summaries by subject or browsing a publication's index or table of contents, in addition to word searching for specific terms within individual documents. If you do not do any pre-search filtering, you will likely have to use word searching.

B. CRITERIA FOR PRE-SEARCH FILTERING ▼

Think back to the spinach manicotti examples from Chapter 1. When you select a recipe for spinach manicotti, any recipe is roughly as good as any other. Your selection from the available choices turns on your individual needs and desires. In the law, however, one source is not as good as any other. For example, the type and weight of a legal authority affects how much attention, if any, you should give it in analyzing a client's situation. If a particular legal rule governs your client's situation, you must find the authority or authorities that contain that rule for your research to be accurate. Therefore, it is important to understand the appropriate criteria for pre-search filtering.

The three most significant criteria affecting your pre-search filtering are jurisdiction, type of authority, and subject area. You know from Chapter 2 that legal rules apply only to conduct occurring within the jurisdiction where the authority is in force. If Ohio is the controlling jurisdiction, you know you need rules from Ohio, not Florida. If you do not know the controlling jurisdiction, you cannot use this as a basis for pre-search filtering and will often have to conduct preliminary research on the question of jurisdiction. Early in your legal studies, your professor is likely to give you some guidance about the controlling jurisdiction. Additionally, a number of secondary sources are not jurisdiction-specific, so you can locate general information about your research question with those sources even if you do not know the controlling jurisdiction.

The type of authority is another significant factor in pre-search filtering. If you know you need a specific form of primary authority, such as cases or statutes, you can limit your search to those sources. If you are not certain but have enough background knowledge to have a sense of the type of primary authority you need, pre-filtering to focus on a specific type of authority can be useful.

If you do not know or do not have a sense of the type of primary authority you need, you cannot use this as a basis for pre-search filtering. You could search for multiple types of primary authority and filter the results by type of authority after you have done some research. Another strategy is focusing initially on secondary sources that provide an overview of the law. This can be an effective way to identify the types of primary authority relevant to your research task, especially if the research question involves more than one type of authority.

Making assumptions about the relevant type of authority can be a trap. Much of the first year of law school focuses on common-law rules, that is, rules developed through cases. This can lead to a tendency to gravitate toward cases when conducting research. Being aware of this trap will help you avoid it. Cases are only one form of authority, and you should not automatically turn to cases as the most relevant type of authority for all research questions.

Pre-filtering by subject area can also help limit the scope of your research. When you identify a research question, you narrow the field of all legal information to that relevant to the subject of your research. If you know the general subject area the question falls into (e.g., torts, civil procedure, intellectual property, employment law, etc.), you can sometimes use that information to focus before you search. For example, some secondary sources are devoted to specific subject areas. If you know you need information on a subject addressed by a specific secondary source, pre-search filtering by subject can lead you to that source. Some online research providers divide their contents by subject category, so you may be able to filter by subject in that way as well. The subject categories in online services can be fairly limited, so pre-search filtering by subject area can be less useful with those services.

Some secondary sources are very general and provide information on a wide range of subject areas. If you are unable to pre-filter by subject area, you might try filtering by type of authority to locate a general secondary source you can use to identify the relevant subject area(s).

You may have additional criteria for focusing your search such as a date or level of court. If you can identify these criteria through pre-search filtering, you can use them to further limit the scope of the information you seek. Often, however, your pre-search filtering will center on some combination of jurisdiction, type of authority, and subject area, with additional criteria used as part of the post-search filtering process.

C. A PROCESS FOR PRE-SEARCH FILTERING ⎯⎯⎯⎯⎯▼

Your goal with pre-search filtering is to use the information you already have to focus your research task before you search for authority. This will determine the level of generality at which to begin your research and set the framework for the research steps you need to follow. Pre-search filtering that focuses on the wrong criteria will send you in the wrong direction in your research. Therefore, as you engage in pre-search filtering, ask yourself why you think you should focus your research according to a particular criterion and how confident you are in your choice. Assessing your confidence might cause you to rethink your choices, and even if that is not the case, will give you a basis for refining your approach as you continue your research. Figure 4.2 shows how you might approach pre-search filtering with the research question from Chapter 3 regarding the neighbor who blew cigar smoke on your client. As a reminder, here are the facts of the scenario:

Your client lives in North Carolina. He lives in a duplex with a front porch that extends across the entire front of the house. Your client's side of the porch is separated from his neighbor's side by a railing. The neighbor likes to smoke cigars on her own front porch, but the smoke travels to the client's front porch. The client told his neighbor that he finds the smell of the smoke intolerable. The neighbor had previously promised not to smoke on her front porch but regularly broke her promise, to the client's great consternation. One day, while the neighbor was smoking on her porch, the client berated her for breaking her promise. The neighbor, without saying a word, leaned over the railing separating the two porches, blew cigar smoke into the client's face, and sat back down on her own porch to finish the cigar. The client is upset about this interaction and wants to know whether he can recover damages from his neighbor.

FIGURE 4.2   Pre-Search Filtering

PRE-SEARCH FILTERING CRITERIA	BASIS FOR FILTERING BY EACH CRITERION	DEGREE OF CONFIDENCE	SEARCH STRATEGY BASED ON DEGREE OF CONFIDENCE
Controlling jurisdiction: *North Carolina*	The events occurred in North Carolina.	*High*	Search for North Carolina authority.
Subject areas: *Torts* *Contracts* *Criminal Law*	*Torts*: Battery and trespass to land are torts.	*High*	Search for information on torts, specifically battery and trespass to land.
	Contracts: Contracts are enforceable promises, and the neighbor broke a promise to the client.	*Medium*: A contract requires more than a promise; the promise in this case may not constitute a contractual obligation.	Search for information on contracts, specifically, the requirements for a promise to create a contractual obligation.
	Criminal law: Battery and trespass are crimes.	*Low*: If the neighbor committed a crime, the state could pursue criminal charges. Holding the neighbor criminally responsible will not give the client the remedy he seeks.	Skip research into criminal law for now.
Type of authority: *Cases*	Torts and contracts are areas of law frequently developed through common-law rules.	*Medium*: The rules probably come from cases, but the relevant legal principles might be difficult to understand by reading cases in a piecemeal fashion.	Focus the initial search on secondary sources to confirm that common-law rules apply and to get an overview of the relevant legal principles. Then search by source for cases if appropriate.

Based on the assessment of the client's situation in Figure 4.3, secondary sources would be a good starting point for your research, although you could start with cases or an unfiltered search if you had enough background knowledge of tort and contract law.

Once you have assessed the information you have about your research question to focus the search as much as possible, you are ready to begin looking for information. To do that, you will need to select a search technique to identify information relevant to your research question. Word searching and other search options are discussed in the next chapter.

Research Tools and Search Techniques

After you finish pre-search filtering, you must decide which research tool(s) you will use to access the information you need and which search technique(s) are most likely to be effective. To a certain extent, these two inquiries cannot be separated. The search techniques available can affect your decision about which research tool to use, and the features of the research tool you use may dictate your search technique. Although these two aspects of research are related, this chapter first explains some considerations in selecting a research tool and then describes search techniques, including different types of word searches.

A. SELECTING A RESEARCH TOOL ▼

Because much legal information is available in multiple formats, you will have to decide how you want to access that information. Research tools that provide access to specific forms of authority are discussed in Part II of this book. This section discusses general categories of research tools and the considerations that can affect which tools you choose for any given research task.

The types of research tools you can use to access legal information can be divided into four categories:

▼ **Print resources**
The holdings in your law library may be the easiest and most cost-effective resources for you to use.

▼ **Fee-based online resources**
These services charge fees for using the service. They include well-known commercial providers like Westlaw, Lexis, and Bloomberg Law. They also include lower-cost services like VersusLaw, Fastcase, Casemaker, and others. The billing structure varies considerably among services, to include flat rates for large organizations or per-search fees to individual users. Some bar associations provide access to Fastcase or Casemaker as

part of bar membership. Some services, such as Casetext, provide a free basic level of service and charge fees for premium levels. All of these services provide access to a wide range of legal authorities.

▼ Online subscription resources

These services charge the subscriber for access, but individual users ordinarily are not charged for researching with the service. Often, these are specialized services that provide access to specific forms of authority or authority in specialized subject areas. Your law library's research portal should list subscription services available to you as a law student.

▼ Publicly available resources

Government websites can provide access to local, state, and federal legal information. Websites operated by trade, civic, educational, or other groups may provide useful information in their specialized fields. A number of free legal research sites collect legal information. For example, FindLaw and Cornell Law School's Legal Information Institute provide access to a wide range of authorities. Google has a specialty search engine called Google Scholar that you can use for free case research.

You want to choose the research tool best suited to your research task. As noted above, one of the main considerations will be the search techniques available. If you want to search in a particular way, you must select a research tool that offers the search option you want. For example, Lexis, Westlaw, and Bloomberg Law allow unfiltered searching. Other services may require you to select a database before you search. If you want to execute an unfiltered search, this will affect your choice of research tool.

Beyond that, you should select the research tool most likely to contain the information you need. You need to consider the type of information you need, the scope of coverage of the resources available to you, and the reliability and currentness of the information. In addition, although you may not be concerned with the cost of research while you are in law school, in practice, selecting a cost-effective resource is also an important consideration.

B. COMMON SEARCH TECHNIQUES: CITATION, WORD, AND SUBJECT SEARCHING _____▼

In conjunction with selecting a research tool, you must decide which search technique(s) are likely to lead you to relevant information. Three common search techniques are retrieving a document from its citation, searching by subject, and executing a word search.

If you have the citation to an authority that is relevant to your research, retrieving that document and using it as an entry point into the research process is an efficient research strategy. The document itself will educate you so that you can expand your search into other sources effectively. The document will also likely cite other legal authorities, which you can read to expand your search. Further, many legal authorities include research notes that can guide you toward other useful information.

Although starting with a relevant citation is great when you have that option, often you will not have citations to relevant authorities at the start of your project. When that is the case, you will have the options of searching by subject or executing a word search. We do so much word searching in daily life that many researchers gravitate toward word searching in legal research. Because a word search looks for terms you identify, it is the most flexible way to search for information. This can be helpful for fact-specific research, such as when you are searching for cases with specific facts similar to the facts of your client's situation, or when the applicable legal concepts are expressed with relatively unique phrasing, such as "negligence per se," a well-known tort doctrine.

But word searches also risk retrieving irrelevant documents or missing important documents. For example, virtually every civil lawsuit is initiated by the filing of a document called a complaint. "Complaint," however, is both a term of art and a common, everyday word. If you wanted to research the requirements for a "complaint," you would want references to the document used to initiate a civil suit, not to the everyday use of the term. Although all concepts must ultimately be expressed in words, a search for the individual terms that express a general concept may not be focused enough to be as effective as a subject search.

Conversely, a word search for a specific term can miss important documents if the concept is described using different terms. For example, a concept in contract law called the "mailbox" rule is also known as the "deposit acceptance" rule and the "postal acceptance" rule. If you searched for one of those terms but not the others, you might miss important information. If some documents in a database use only one of the alternative terms, the search would not retrieve them.

Searching by subject is another way to conduct legal research. In print, you can search by subject using the table of contents or index to a publication to find information within that publication. The index will usually contain more detail than the table of contents, and because it is organized by subject, will contain cross-references to related material. Some online services provide access to the tables of contents or indexes of selected publications, and you can use those the same way you would in print. Online services also often offer specialized subject-searching tools that provide a directory of subject area topics.

One advantage to subject searching is that if the concept you are researching is described with commonly used words, an index or other subject compilation will reference only significant discussions of the concept, not every occurrence of everyday terms. Subject-searching tools like an index prioritize the information within a source to help direct you to the most important information. Thus, an entry for "complaint" in an index will refer you to information on the document used to initiate a lawsuit, not the term as used in an everyday sense.

Another advantage of subject searching is that index cross-references will point you in the right direction if you look up terms that are close to, but perhaps not exactly on point with, the topic you are researching. Returning to the "mailbox" rule example, if you knew about the "mailbox" rule but did not know the alternative terms "deposit acceptance" and "postal acceptance" rule, an index entry for the "mailbox" rule would likely cross-reference entries under the other terms.

On the other hand, if you want to search for terms or topics that do not appear in an index or subject compilation, subject-searching tools will not lead you to the information you need. And if the publisher has compiled the material using topic names that are completely unfamiliar to you, you may not be able to find index or subject entries that are helpful.

Specialized subject-searching tools unique to specific types of authority are discussed in Part II, which is devoted to individual forms of authority. Techniques for effective word searches in virtually any online service are discussed below.

C. EFFECTIVE WORD SEARCHING _____▼

1. Types of Word Searches

When you execute a word search, the search engine searches a database of documents and retrieves the documents that meet the criteria you set for the search. To do this, the search engine uses an algorithm, or set of rules, to evaluate the search criteria and the documents in the database. There are three types of word searches: terms and connectors (also called Boolean), natural language, and descriptive term. Although you get similar search results with each type of word search, the results are not exactly the same, so you should understand some of the differences among these options.

A terms and connectors search is a literal search. It identifies documents containing the precise terms in your word search, in the precise relationships you specify. For example, you could search for documents that contain both the phrase **"ice cream"** and the term **sundae**. Alternatively, you could search for documents that contain either the phrase **"ice cream"** or the term **sundae**, but not necessarily both. **AND** and **OR** are examples of connectors, which are the commands that define the relationships among the search terms.

You can control the search results more precisely with terms and connectors searching than you can with other types of word searching because you use commands to steer the search logic. If you search for **"ice cream" AND sundae**, the search will retrieve only documents that contain the phrase **"ice cream"** and the term **sundae**; if a document contains **"ice cream"** but not **sundae**, or **sundae** but not **"ice cream"**, that document will not appear in the search results. The search may retrieve any number of documents, or no documents at all, depending on the number of documents that meet the search criteria. Lexis, Westlaw, and most other online services allow terms and connectors searching; some use it exclusively. More information on specific terms and connectors commands appears below.

A natural language search is also a literal search. It identifies documents containing the precise terms in your search. But unlike a terms and connectors search, a natural language search does not require you to specify the relationships among the terms. Instead, a natural language search uses embedded rules to evaluate the relationships among the search terms, which it then uses to determine which documents meet the search criteria. A natural language search for **ice cream sundae** will retrieve documents that contain all or some of those terms and will rank the results by relevance. Documents in which the terms appear frequently or close together will be ranked higher than documents that contain only one of the search terms.

A descriptive term search, as that term is used in this book, refers to a variation of natural language searching that is nonliteral. It uses embedded rules to evaluate which documents meet the search criteria, but it searches both the text of the documents in the database and metadata associated with the documents. In addition to retrieving documents that contain the search terms, therefore, it can also retrieve documents that appear relevant according to the embedded search rules even though they do not contain the search terms. It is extremely rare for a descriptive term search to retrieve no documents. Westlaw and Google Scholar have descriptive term search engines.

2. Drafting Effective Word Searches

When you draft any type of word search, you should follow three steps:

- Develop the initial search terms.
- Expand the breadth and depth of the search.
- Prioritize terms to identify those you will use in your initial search and those you will save for subsequent searches or post-search filtering. (The process of post-search filtering is addressed in the next chapter.)

You should have already developed a list of search terms in conjunction with articulating a research question, as described in Chapter 3. Think about the problem in terms of the parties, any places or things, potential claims and defenses, and the relief sought.

Having identified the relevant terms, your next step is expanding the search. Recall that most word searches are literal. If an object, idea, concept, or action is expressed in a document using terms different from your search terms, a literal search will not locate the document. Unless you are searching for terms of art that need to appear precisely for a document to be useful, you need to expand the breadth and depth of the search. As Chapter 3 explains, expanding the breadth of the search involves generating synonyms and terms related to the initial search terms, as well as varying the degree of abstraction with which you express the concepts in the search.

Although you can execute a search with many terms, an overly complex search may not accomplish your research goals. Therefore, once you have developed and expanded the search terms, the next step is prioritizing them. Do this by categorizing the search terms. One category might be terms describing the people or objects in the search. Another might be terms describing action or conduct. A third might be terms describing applicable legal doctrines. If one category is more important to your research than others, you may want to include several alternative terms in that category in your initial search and save terms in other categories for later searches. If terms in two or more categories are critical, edit your initial list to reflect the terms you think are most likely to appear in relevant documents, expressed at the appropriate degree of abstraction for your search.

3. Terms and Connectors Searching

Terms and connectors searching is useful as an initial search strategy when you want to control the relationships among the search terms. Additionally, terms and connectors is the form of searching you often must use during post-search filtering when you execute a narrowing search within the initial search results. Therefore, you need to understand how to use terms and connectors searching.

a. Terms and Connectors Search Logic

In terms and connectors searching, you define the relationships among the terms in the search using connectors and other commands. Figure 5.1 lists the most commonly used commands. In many services, you can type terms and connectors commands into the search box or construct a terms and connectors search using advanced search options.

▼ **FIGURE 5.1**   Common Terms and Connectors Commands

Alternative terms	Term1 **or** Term2
All terms	Term1 **and** Term2
Terms with grammatical proximity	Term1 **/p** Term2 (Term1 appears within the same paragraph as Term2) Term1 **/s** Term2 (Term1 appears within the same sentence as Term2)
Terms with numerical proximity	Term1 **/n** Term2 (Term1 appears within a certain number of words of Term2; *n* = a specific number)
Exclude terms	*Westlaw, Bloomberg Law:* Term1 **but not** Term2 *Lexis, Bloomberg Law:* Term1 **and not** Term2
Expand terms	*Westlaw, Bloomberg Law:* Exclamation point (!) for variable word endings (Term! retrieves Term, Terms, Termed, Terming, Terminal, Terminable, and all other variations of the word) *Bloomberg Law:* Exclamation point to substitute for multiple variable letters (S!holder retrieves Shareholder and Stockholder) *Westlaw:* Asterisk (*) to substitute for variable individual letters (Te*m retrieves Term, Team, and Teem) *Lexis:* Asterisk (*) or exclamation point (!) for variable word endings (Term* and Term! retrieve Term, Terms, Termed, Terming, Terminal, Terminable, and all other variations of the word) *Lexis:* Asterisk (*) to substitute for multiple variable letters (S*holder retrieves Shareholder and Stockholder) *Lexis:* Asterisk (*) or question mark (?) to substitute for variable individual letters (Te*m and Te?m retrieve Term, Team, and Teem)

Most searches contain several terms and may contain multiple connectors. When the search is executed, the search engine uses Boolean logic to process the connectors in a specific sequence. For example, in Westlaw and Lexis, the **OR** connector is processed first, followed by the numerical and grammatical proximity connectors (**/N, /P, /S**), the **AND** connector, and finally, the exclusion connectors (**AND NOT, BUT NOT**).

If you search for **ice AND cream OR sundae,** Westlaw and Lexis would process the search for the terms **cream OR sundae** first. After documents with one or the other of those terms were identified, the search for the term **ice** would begin. In effect, the query would be processed as a search for the terms **ice AND cream, OR,** in the alternative, the terms **ice AND sundae.** If this was not the intended search, it could miss documents containing the terms you want or retrieve irrelevant documents.

The hierarchy of connectors is not uniform across services. Bloomberg Law, for example, processes connectors in the order in which they appear in the search. It is important to know the hierarchy of connectors in any service you use to search effectively.

It is possible to modify a search to vary the operation of the connectors. One way is by creating a search phrase instead of placing a connector between terms. Often you can do this by placing terms in quotation marks: **"ice cream"** instead of **ice AND cream.** Another way is to segregate the **ice AND cream** portion of the search. Often, you can accomplish this by placing a portion of the search in parentheses: **(ice AND cream) OR sundae.** The terms within parentheses would be treated as a separate unit. Thus, the **AND** connector would apply only to the terms within the parentheses. In this example, adding parentheses would result in a search for the terms **ice AND cream** as a unit, and then in the alternative, for the individual term **sundae.**

b. Drafting a Terms and Connectors Search

The three steps described above for drafting effective word searches apply to terms and connectors searches: develop the initial list of terms, expand the list, and prioritize the terms. With a terms and connectors search, however, you must also incorporate the appropriate search commands.

In the first step, one way you can expand the breadth of the search terms is by using term expanders. These may include the asterisk (*) to substitute for individual letters and the exclamation point (!) to substitute for variable word endings. (Although many services use term expander characters, the functions of the characters are not standard. For example, the asterisk in some services is used for variable word endings, not the exclamation point. You should review the search commands in any service if you are not familiar with them.)

Once you have developed and expanded the search terms, the next step is specifying the appropriate relationships among the terms using connectors. Grouping search terms by category will help you identify the appropriate connectors. You will typically want to search within each category for synonyms or related terms in the alternative, so you will likely use **OR** to connect those terms.

Among the categories of terms, you'll use different connectors. The closer the connections you require among the categories, the more restrictive the search will be. The broader the connections, the more open the search will be. For example, the **AND** connector, which requires only that both words appear somewhere within the same document, will retrieve more documents than a proximity connector such as **/P**, which requires the words to appear within the same paragraph. Be sure to take the hierarchy of connectors into account as you consider the relationships among the search terms. If necessary, use parentheses to group terms that you want to search together.

In addition to allowing you to search for terms within the body of a document, many services will allow you to limit your search to individual components of the document, such as words in the title or the name of the author. Although you will not always use this search option, it is an important feature to understand.

Document components may be called "fields," "segments," or something similar. Westlaw and Lexis will allow you to add field or segment restrictions by typing special commands into the search box or by using advanced search menu options. For example, if you needed to find all opinions written by former Chief Justice William Rehnquist, a search for his name in a case law database would retrieve tens of thousands of documents. You could limit the search to opinions he wrote with the Written By field or segment.

Although you can make a terms and connectors search very specific by using multiple search commands, an effective terms and connectors search does not have to use all or even most of the available commands. The structure and complexity of any search will depend on the nature of the information you need. The important thing is to know what the commands are so you can use them to steer the search engine to retrieve information relevant to your research task.

4. Example Searches

To see how to use the process of drafting an effective word search, assume your client lost her pet macaw, Marigold, when the bird escaped from its enclosure and flew away. A neighbor captured the macaw and refuses to return it. The issue is who owns Marigold now.

An initial list of search terms would likely include the following: **macaw, owner, escape**. You can expand the breadth and depth of that initial list as follows:

- The subject of the search — **macaw** — can be expressed more concretely as **Marigold,** the specific macaw at issue. Of course, that term is too concrete to be useful; authority involving macaws named Marigold does not likely exist. Instead, you should express the term more abstractly as **bird, pet, animal,** or **property**.
- The actions that describe what happened — **escape** and **capture** — can be expressed in a slightly different context with the related terms **lost, found, catch,** and **trap**.
- Your client's status as **owner** is another relevant search term.

In a natural language or descriptive term search, you can execute a search with some or all of those terms. You would want to prioritize terms to focus on what is most important in your research. For example, if you need authority specifically related to birds, then **bird** needs to be in the initial search. This client's situation, however, lends itself to a search for more general concepts. The applicable rules for birds probably are not different than those for other types of pets. You could start with the terms **animal or pet**. You would want to include the term **owner** to reflect your client's status. The alternatives to **escape** and **capture** are such common terms that you might not include them in an initial search, saving them for post-search filtering. The initial search might look like this:

animal pet escape capture owner

Depending on what the search retrieves, you could use different or additional terms as part of your post-search filtering. If the initial search yields little information, you could search again using the most general term (**property**); if it retrieved too many documents, you could narrow the results using the most specific term (**bird**). Reviewing the initial search results might introduce you to the term **replevin**, which is the name of an action seeking return of personal property.

In a terms and connectors search, you would need to specify the relationships among the terms. Working from the groups of terms, those relating to Marigold should be connected with **OR** because they are alternative ways of identifying the macaw:

animal or pet

Another category describes what happened to Marigold. These terms can be expressed as alternatives connected with **OR**. You would likely use root expanders to capture the variations on the terms (escape, escaped, escaping; capture, captured, capturing):

escap! or captur!

A third category describes your client's status. The term **owner** has variations that could be relevant to the search. Again, you would likely use the term with a root expander to capture the variations on the word (owner, ownership):

owner!

The next step is specifying the relationships among the categories of terms. Terms relating to the subject of the dispute and those describing what happened can be connected with **AND** because you would want the results to reflect both aspects of the problem. The term **owner!** could be connected to the terms **pet or animal** using a more restrictive connector, such as **/P**, to help limit the context to situations relevant to your client's situation. Here is what the search might look like:

pet or animal /p owner! and escap! or captur!

This is not the only way to create this search. You could use different terms or express the relationships among terms differently. As with natural language and descriptive term searching, think about layering your search to prioritize the most important terms and save others for post-search filtering.

Try these searches and some variations on them for yourself to see what authority you find in the state of New York (or any other jurisdiction your professor specifies). What rule determines whether an animal that escapes is returned to its original owner?

Working with Search Results

After you locate information, you need to assess the search results in a way that allows you to determine whether you have found what you need, or if not, what additional steps you should take to identify the relevant information. You might need to view a list of documents, read the text of individual documents, find specific terms within a document, or use links to other documents. If you have located a large number of documents, you might also need to limit or filter the results to focus on the information most relevant to your research task. Once you have found useful information, you need to make sure that information is up to date, and you will often need to repeat the search process to locate more or better information.

A. ASSESSING SEARCH RESULTS ▼

1. The Organization of the Results

In assessing your search results, it is important to pay attention to how the information is organized. When you search online, the default display order is often by relevance. Depending on the source and search technique used, however, the information can be organized differently. Cases are commonly listed in reverse date order, statutes in numerical order, and secondary sources in alphabetical order. Because Internet search engines usually use relevancy rankings, we have been conditioned to review only the first several items in the results to assess the effectiveness of a search. If your results are displayed in a different order, however, the best information could be in the middle or at the end of the results.

If the results are organized by relevance, documents with the best match to your search criteria appear first. Relevance, however, is a relative concept. A document is likely to be deemed more relevant if the search terms appear frequently or close to each other in the document. The precise criteria for determining relevance varies by information provider, and the relevancy ranking of documents retrieved from the same search may vary depending on which service you use. You should treat the rankings as an approximation that cannot substitute for your own judgment about the relevance of the documents the search retrieves.

The most useful order for displaying search results will depend on your research task. Relevancy ranking is useful when the search retrieves a large number of documents. Date order may be better if you are looking for the most recent authority on an issue. Often you will have the option to change the default order (from date to relevance or from relevance to alphabetical, depending on the source). Regardless of whether you can change the default setting, you must be aware of the order in which the documents are listed to assess the effectiveness of the search.

2. Telling Things Apart Online

The beauty of online research is that you can view virtually any type of authority on a single screen. Because all information appears in the same format, however, it can be hard to tell one source from another. In law, as you know, one source is not as good as any other, so being aware of what you are viewing is critical to evaluating your search results.

An example illustrates how different forms of authority can look the same online. You may have seen Instagram or Facebook postings through which users attempt to assert privacy rights over their posted content. A typical notice contains the following language that references the Uniform Commercial Code (UCC):

> I do not give Instagram or any entities associated with Facebook permission to use my pictures, information, messages or posts, both past and future. With this statement, I give notice to Instagram it is strictly forbidden to disclose, copy, distribute, or take any other action against me based on this profile and/or its contents. The content of this profile is private and confidential information. The violation of privacy can be punished by law (UCC 1-308, 1-103).

If you wanted to investigate the validity of this notice, you could begin by researching UCC 1-103.[1] Figure 6.1 contains snippets from three sources regarding UCC 1-103. See if you can tell the differences among them.

---

1. In fact, the Instagram and Facebook terms of service govern users' privacy rights, and the UCC provisions cited are not relevant in this context. This is one of many Internet hoaxes that circulate periodically. *See www.snopes.com.*

▼ **FIGURE 6.1**   UCC 1-103 Information

A.

336.1-103 CONSTRUCTION OF UNIFORM COMMERCIAL CODE TO PROMOTE ITS PURPOSES AND POLICIES; APPLICABILITY OF SUPPLEMENTAL PRINCIPLES OF LAW.

(a) The Uniform Commercial Code must be liberally construed and applied to promote its underlying purposes and policies, which are:

(1) to simplify, clarify, and modernize the law governing commercial transactions;

(2) to permit the continued expansion of commercial practices through custom, usage, and agreement of the parties; and

(3) to make uniform the law among the various jurisdictions.

(b) Unless displaced by the particular provisions of the Uniform Commercial Code, the principles of law and equity, including the law merchant and the law relative to capacity to contract, principal and agent, estoppel, fraud, misrepresentation, duress, coercion, mistake, bankruptcy, and other validating or invalidating cause supplement its provisions.

History: *2004 c 162 art 1 s 3*

B.

Even though the UCC does not supplant all the law applicable to commercial transactions, it is still the primary source of the commercial law rules for the areas it governs because it represents the considered choices of its drafters and of the Tennessee General Assembly about the appropriate policies to be furthered in the transactions it covers. *See* UCC § 1-103 cmt. 2 (revised 2001). 1 U.L.A. 11 (2004). The purposes and policies reflected in the UCC include (a) symplifying, clarifying, and modernizing the law governing commercial transactions, (b) permitting the continued expansion of commercial practices through custom, usage, and agreement of the parties, *281 and (c) making uniform the law among the various jurisdictions. Tenn. Code Ann. § 47-1-102(2). Thus, while generally applicable principles of law and equity can be used to supplement the UCC, they may not be used to supplant the UCC's provisions or the purposes or policies these provisions reflect. UCC § 1-103 cmt. 2 (revised 2001), 1 U.L.A. 11 (2004); 1 JAMES J. WHITE & ROBERT S. SUMMERS, UNIFORM COMMERCIAL CODE § 1-C, at 7 (5th ed. 2006) (analyzing the comments to the 2001 revisions to Article 1).

C.

The term UCC is short for Uniform Commercial Code.

The Uniform Commercial Code represents a general and comprehensive revision of the state's prior laws applicable to commercial transactions. The Code provides a uniform and easily available set of rules for the conduct of commercial transactions responsive to modern business conditions and needs. In short, the purpose was to simplify, clarify and modernize the law(s) governing commercial transactions; to make uniform the law among the various jurisdictions, and to permit the continued expansion of commercial practices through custom, usage, and agreement of the parties involved. [*Parts taken from the McKinney's Consolidated Laws of New York, Uniform Commercial Code, Book 62.5, Sections 7-101 to End.*]

The items in Figure 6.1 look much the same, but they are really quite different. The first one is a Minnesota statute, the second one is a Tennessee case interpreting a Tennessee statute, and the third one is an explanation of the UCC provided by the New York Department of State. Even though all three authorities include similar information, it would be a serious mistake to treat them as interchangeable in advising a client. If each said something different, treating them as equivalent would increase the risk of giving a client bad advice.

With print research, a researcher has to physically move from one location to another and use different books to research different forms of authority from different jurisdictions. This makes the person aware in a physical sense of the differences among forms of authority. With online research, a case or statute from one jurisdiction looks the same as a case or a statute from another jurisdiction. Even within a single jurisdiction, cases from different levels of court or statutes applicable to different subject areas look the same. Therefore, when you search online, you must pay close attention to the material you find to assess whether it is primary or secondary authority and whether it is binding or nonbinding.

When you select a jurisdiction or type of authority to research, you are likely to keep the status of the authority in mind as you review what you have found. As you follow links within documents, however, it is easy to lose track of the weight or status of a document you are reading, especially if you are only reading snippets of each document (like the ones in Figure 6.1) before moving on. Additionally, if your pre-search filtering does not give you a basis for selecting a jurisdiction or type of authority, the search results will contain many different forms of authority, some of which may be binding and some of which may not.

Therefore, as you review your research results online, you must make a point of determining the weight and status of each document you review. The easiest way to do this is to review the heading of the document. Virtually every information provider puts a heading at the top of each document with a citation you can use to determine the document's weight. If you are not sure about the weight of an authority, you should make a note to check that as part of your updating process. If you find something useful that is not binding, you should make a note to that effect. More information on note taking appears in Chapter 7, but taking the time to make sure you understand what you are reading is critical to assessing your search results regardless of how you keep track of your research.

3. Post-Search Filtering

Filtering the search results will help you assess how effective the search was. Generally, the more effective your pre-search filtering, the less post-search filtering you will need to do. If you find little information on your research question, you might read everything you can find that seems relevant without filtering the results at all. Usually, however, you will need to engage in at least some post-search filtering to isolate the best authority from the search, meaning the authority that most closely meets your needs.

Post-search filtering criteria can be divided into two categories:

- general document characteristics;
- specific content.

These categories reflect the considerations that would cause you to prefer one document or set of documents over another: the authorities' relative weight and factual relevance to your research question. You might use multiple criteria to filter a search that retrieves many documents or only one criterion to focus on a specific type of document, depending on the goal of your search.

General document characteristics include jurisdiction and type of authority (e.g., cases, statutes, secondary sources). If you did not or were not able to filter by these criteria as part of your pre-search filtering, you can use these criteria for post-search filtering. You may also be able to filter the results according to other general document characteristics such as date, level of court (for cases), or publication or author (for secondary sources).

Specific content is another way to filter content after a search. Sometimes you can filter the results by subject. If the type of document you are researching includes research notes organized by subject, you may be able to filter the results according to those subject categories to target the documents most relevant to your research. For example, many cases include research notes called headnotes that summarize the main points in the opinion. You can often narrow your search by headnote subject to focus on the most relevant cases. More information on headnote searching appears in Chapter 9.

When you search online, another way to narrow the results for specific content is by searching for terms within the documents. With this option, you execute a word search within the search results to isolate documents that contain the terms you specify. Even if you use natural language or descriptive term searching for your initial search, a search within search results will almost always be a terms and connectors search. (More information on terms and connectors searching appears in Chapter 5.)

The way you draft the narrowing search will depend on how you want to filter the search results. Three ways you might want to narrow search results include:

- adding terms that were not part of the initial search;
- focusing on particular terms that were part of the initial search;
- changing the relationships among terms that were part of the initial search.

The results of your initial search will depend in part on the level of abstraction of your search terms. If you execute a broad search for a general concept, you will likely retrieve many documents. You may want to narrow the results by adding more specific terms. For example, assumption of risk is a defense to a negligence claim. If you were researching assumption of risk in the context of rock climbing accidents, you might begin your research by looking more abstractly for material related to assumption of risk in sports or recreation. If that search retrieved too many documents to be useful, you could then execute a narrowing search for authority that specifically discusses rock climbing.

To use terms and connectors commands effectively in this context, the narrowing search could include **"rock climbing"** as a search phrase. You could also search for the terms in proximity to one another with a term expander to capture variations on the word **climb**. Thus, the narrowing search might look like this:

rock /5 climb!

This search would retrieve documents in which the term **rock** appears within five words before or after any variation of the word **climb** (climb, climbed, climber, climbing, climbs).

Another way to narrow the search results is by focusing on terms that were part of your initial search. If you execute a search for several alternative terms and retrieve too many documents, narrowing the search to focus on one or two specific terms will limit the search results.

A third way to narrow the search results is to use search connectors and commands to change the relationships among the terms in the initial search. The **AND** connector will limit the results by identifying documents that contain all of the specific terms instead of only one. Using the numerical or grammatical connectors (/N, /P, /S) to target documents that contain the terms close together is another good strategy. The exclusion connectors (**AND NOT, BUT NOT**) are useful when you have a term that is relevant when used in one context but not relevant in others. By excluding documents that contain terms associated with the irrelevant context, you can target more relevant documents. You can also use search commands to search for terms only within the title or other specific component of the document (e.g., using a field or segment search in Westlaw or Lexis).

B. UPDATING RESEARCH ▼

The law, of course, can change at any time. New cases are decided; older cases can be overruled; statutes can be enacted, amended, or repealed. Therefore, an essential step in evaluating your search results is making sure the information is current. One way to update your research is with a specialized research tool called a citator, which is explained in Chapter 10. In addition, most sources of legal information will indicate how recently they have been updated to help you assess whether the information is current.

Most print research sources consist of hardcover books that can be difficult to update when the law changes. Some print resources, such as case reporters, are published in chronological order. For those resources, new books are published periodically as new material is compiled. Many, however, are organized by subject. For those resources, publishers cannot print new books every time the law changes. This would be prohibitively expensive, and because the law can change at any time, the new books would likely be out of date as soon as they were printed. To keep the books current, therefore, many print sources are updated with softcover pamphlets containing new information that becomes available after the hardcover book is published. This type of pamphlet is called a "pocket part" because it fits into a pocket in the inside back cover of the hardcover book. The hardcover book and the pocket part will indicate the period of time each covers.

Online sources also usually contain publication or revision date information that you can use to assess how current any information is. Online sources can be updated easily in the sense that new information can be added and older information revised at any time and as frequently as necessary. Westlaw, Lexis, and Bloomberg Law update some of their content on a daily basis. Providers other than major commercial services may not update their content as frequently. In addition, updates for some content only become available when the print version of the source is updated, which means the online version is only as current as the latest print version. Therefore, whether you conduct research in print or online, you must pay careful attention to the date of the information you locate.

C. REFINING, REPEATING, AND ENDING THE SEARCH ___▼

As noted throughout this book, research is a recursive process. A single search is unlikely to retrieve exactly what you need, unless you are retrieving a document from its citation. More often, after you conduct some research, you will return to earlier steps in the process, using what you have learned to refine the process further. As one information provider explains:

> Searching is a process, not an event. This should be your mantra when [conducting research]. . . . After each query, evaluate its success by asking:
>
> - Did I find what I was looking for?
> - What better information could still be out there?
> - How can I refine my query to find better information?[2]

---

2. VersusLaw, Inc. Research Manual, Part I, Electronic Searching Strategy, *www.versuslaw.com*; *select* Help, Research Manual, Research Manual Part 1 — Search Basics (accessed October 11, 2019).

As you filter the information from your search, evaluate what you have found with an eye toward refining the search. Based on what you find, you may revise the types of information you need, the relevant terms or subject areas, or both. Be prepared to repeat the search process until you have isolated the subset of legal information necessary to answer your research question.

1. Is Your Research Complete?

Although you will almost always have to refine and repeat your search to find all the information you need, at some point you have to stop. Deciding when your research is complete can be difficult. The more research you do, the more comfortable you will be with the process, and the more you will develop an internal sense of when a project is complete. In your first few research assignments in law school, however, you will probably feel uncertain about when to stop because you will have little prior experience to draw upon in making that decision.

One issue that affects a person's sense of when to stop is personal work style. Some people are anxious to begin writing and therefore stop researching after they locate a few sources that seem relevant. Others put off writing by continuing to research, thinking that the answer will become apparent if they just keep looking a little bit more. Being aware of your work style will help you determine whether you have stopped too soon or are continuing your research beyond what is necessary for the assignment.

Of course, the amount of time you have and the work product you are expected to produce will affect the ending point for your research. If you are instructed to report back in half an hour with your research results, you know when you will need to stop. In general, however, you will know that you have come full circle in your research when, after following a comprehensive research path through a variety of sources, the authorities you locate start to refer back to each other and the new sources you consult fail to reveal significant new information.

The fact that a few of the sources you have located appear relevant does not mean it is time to stop researching. Until you have explored other potential research avenues, you should continue your work. It might be that the authorities you initially locate will turn out to be the most relevant, but you cannot have confidence in that result until you research additional authorities. On the other hand, you can always keep looking for one more case or one more article to support your analysis, but at some point the benefit of continuing to research will be too small to justify the additional effort. It is unlikely that one magical source exists that is going to resolve your research question. If the answer to the question were clear, you probably would not have been asked to research it.

If you developed a comprehensive research strategy and followed it until you came full circle in your research, it is probably time to stop.

2. What if You Do Not Find Anything Useful?

Even if you follow an organized research plan, from time to time, you will not be able to find what you need. If you have researched several different sources and are unable to find anything, it is time to take a different approach. You should not expect the material you need to appear effortlessly, and blind alleys are inevitable if you approach a problem creatively. Nevertheless, if you find that you really cannot locate any information on an issue, consider the following possibilities:

▼ **Make sure you understand the problem**
One possibility is that you have misunderstood a critical aspect of the problem. If diligent research truly yields nothing useful, you might want to go back to the person who gave you the assignment to make sure you correctly noted all of the factual information you need and have understood the assignment correctly.

▼ **Rethink your search terms**
Have you expanded the breadth and depth of your search terms? You might be researching the right concepts but not have expressed them in a way that yields useful information. Try using synonyms or related terms. If your search terms are concrete, expand your search by using more abstract terms. For example, if you cannot find authority that specifically discusses rock climbing accidents, consider looking more broadly for authority on sports or recreation. Conversely, if your terms are abstract, try using concrete terms to search more narrowly. For example, if you searched unsuccessfully using "moving vehicle" as a search term, try more concrete terms, such as automobile or car.

In addition, you might need to rethink search terms directed to applicable legal theories. If you have focused on a legal theory for which you have not been able to locate authority, you might need to think about other ways to approach the problem. Try not to become so wedded to a legal theory that you pursue it to the exclusion of other viable claims or defenses.

▼ **Use secondary sources**
If you did not consult secondary sources originally, you might want to take that route to find the information you need. The material on the issue might be scattered through many subject areas or statutory sections so that it is difficult to compile the relevant subset of information without secondary sources that tie disparate threads of authority together. In addition, the search terms that seemed applicable when you started your

research might, in fact, not be helpful. Secondary sources can help point you in the right direction.

Another possibility is that you might be looking for the wrong type of authority or in the wrong jurisdiction. Reassess your pre-search filtering to see if you should research in a different jurisdiction or look for a different type of authority. Secondary sources can help you determine which types of primary authority are likely to be relevant to the situation.

Finally, secondary sources can help you determine whether you are facing a question of first impression. If the controlling jurisdiction simply has not faced this question yet, secondary sources should direct you to jurisdictions that have. If no jurisdiction has resolved the issue, secondary sources that analyze the law might identify arguments you can make for resolving the question.

3. What if You Find an Overwhelming Amount of Information?

The same strategies that will help you if you are unable to find anything will also help if you find an overwhelming amount of information. Making sure you understand the problem, of course, is critical. Rethinking your search terms to narrow your approach can also help. If you located information primarily using word searches, you might want to try searching by subject, and vice versa. Consulting secondary sources, however, is probably the most useful strategy. Synthesizing large amounts of authority is difficult. Secondary sources can help you identify the key authorities and otherwise limit the scope of the information on the issue.

Another consideration here is the scope of your research. If much of the authority you have located is secondary authority or nonbinding primary authority, you might need to refocus on binding primary authority from the controlling jurisdiction. If the controlling jurisdiction has a sufficient amount of authority for thorough analysis of the question, you might not need nonbinding authority. You might also need to narrow the scope of your research by limiting the legal theories you are considering. If some are clearly more viable than others and you already have an overwhelming amount of authority, you might want to focus on the theories that seem to provide your client with the best chances of prevailing.

Even when you take these steps, finding an overwhelming amount of material is common with unfiltered searches in Westlaw, Lexis, and Bloomberg Law. Because the results include many types of authority and because of the way search algorithms work, it is not unusual for a search to return thousands or tens of thousands of documents. This is obviously too much information to be useful.

In this situation, using the relevancy rankings and filtering the search results are critical. Although you should not assume that the very best authority will be the first item in the search results, you must rely to some extent on the relevancy rankings when a search retrieves 10,000 documents. Those at the bottom of the list are not likely to be very relevant; they may contain only one reference to only one of your search terms. Post-search filtering is also important. Even when you pre-filter by jurisdiction, you may retrieve both state and related federal information or cases from all levels of court within the state. Limiting the results to the controlling tribunal or a specific publication, using a date restriction, and searching for terms within the initial results are all good strategies for focusing on the most relevant information.

Keeping Track of What You Find

Keeping effective notes as you work is important for several reasons. It will make your research more efficient. You will know where you have already looked, so you can avoid repeating research steps unnecessarily. This is especially critical if you will be working on the project for an extended period of time or if you are working with other people in completing the research. You will also have all the information you need for proper citations. Moreover, if it happens that your project presents novel or complex questions for which there are no definitive answers, careful note taking will allow you to demonstrate that you undertook comprehensive research to try to answer those questions.

Note taking is an individualized process, and there is no single right way to do it. Some online services will keep track of your research by collecting a list of searches you run and documents you view. You may be able to name and save a record of your searches. This is useful, but unless you conduct all of your research with a single research service, it will not be a complete record of your search process. You may be able to download your search history so that you can integrate information from multiple services into a single record of your own, which you can then annotate with your own notes about steps that did and did not lead to useful information.

Once you begin locating specific authorities, you will need to organize what you find. Online services may allow you to create folders for research projects. You can also create your own folders outside of any research service to collect information on your project. Many students use Excel spreadsheets so they can sort information by various criteria such as type of authority, jurisdiction, or date. Online tools for organizing research, such as PowerNotes, Zotero, or Evernote, can be useful.

When you save or download documents, you may want to add notes to them. Online services may have functions that allow you to add sticky notes with comments about the document as a whole. You may also be able to highlight or mark text and append notes at particular locations within a document. You can also do these things without using a research service's tools. Free and inexpensive sticky note software is available, and many programs have commenting functions you can use to add notes to documents.

When you find useful information, you must decide how to organize your research, which documents or snippets to save, and what notes to add to what you have saved. You will probably want to begin by making a folder for all material related to the project as a whole. Sub-folders for research materials, your notes, and any factual documents related to the project may be useful. With respect to research materials, you may want to segregate content by issue if you are researching multiple issues or by type of authority if you are researching a single issue.

When it comes to saving documents, there is a constant tension between stopping to read what you find and saving the document for later. Most people save more than they need, and many students use collecting and saving documents as a procrastination technique, promising themselves that they will read the information later. Excessive downloading or printing will not improve your research. Certainly, having access to key authorities is important for accurate analysis, quotation, and citation. Facing a huge, disorganized collection of information, however, can be demoralizing, especially because most of the information will probably prove to be irrelevant in the end if you have not made thoughtful choices about what to save.

The fact is that you will not know for certain at the beginning of your research which authorities you should save and which you should not. Only as you begin to understand the contours of the legal issue will the relevance (or irrelevance) of individual legal authorities become apparent to you. Therefore, you should conduct some research before you begin saving material. As you delve into the research, you may find that you need to go back to materials you bypassed originally. You may also find it helpful to have a "maybe" folder for your research where you can collect authorities that you are not sure will be helpful. If you do this, however, it is important to return to that information periodically to assess its usefulness.

When you find information you want to save, you may be able to choose between saving the entire document or just a snippet. The benefit of saving a snippet is that you have the precise content that appears relevant.

Saving snippets also presents several potential pitfalls. The passage that seemed most relevant to you at one time may not turn out to be the best part of the document upon later reflection. You also run the risk of taking a passage out of context and representing it inaccurately in your analysis. If you save only snippets, you may be tempted to use a collection of snippets pasted into a document as a substitute for synthesis of the authorities. This can also lead to inadvertent plagiarism if each snippet is not properly cited.

There are times when just a snippet will do, such as when only a few pages out of a lengthy document are relevant to your research. You should be cautious, however, when choosing to save only snippets of documents. Often the better practice is saving the entire document even if you do not plan to use the entire document to analyze your research question.

The next step in documenting your research is deciding which notes to add to the item you save. For most items you will want to note the following information:

Citation	You need this information for two reasons: First, it will force you to pay attention to the status and weight of the authority so you can determine whether it is binding or nonbinding. Even if you use an online service that includes this information automatically when you save the document, you should note it yourself anyway so that you take account of the document's authoritative value.
	Second, if you use your research in a written document, you will need this information to cite your work properly. The information you put in your research notes does not need to be in proper citation form, but enough information for a proper citation should be included here. Note that citations provided by publishers often are not in the proper format for inclusion in a legal document.
Method of locating the document	This could include references to a secondary source that led you to this authority or the search terms you used in an index or database. Noting this information will help you assess which search approaches are most effective. A sticky note or comment at the beginning of the document is a good place to record this information.
The database or source for the document	If you use a folder in an online service, you may not need to note this. If you create your own folder or import content from another source, you should note where you located the item.
Summary of relevant information	This might be a few sentences or a few paragraphs depending on the document and its relevance. Making a note about why you saved the item may jog your memory about its relevance when you go back to review it later, especially if you put the document into a "maybe" file.

Updating information	Note whether the document has been updated and the method of updating. If you are researching in print, you should note the date of any pocket part or supplement.

This might not be the only information you need to note. If you search by subject, you might want to note the most useful subject categories you used. You also might want to make notes or highlight text within the body of a document to make the relevant portions easy for you to find. At a minimum, however, you should keep track of the pieces of information listed above.

Although many people keep notes in digital form and download most of their research material, some people still do better with hard copy. The physical acts of printing important sources, organizing them under tabs in a binder or stacking them in piles on the floor, and marking key portions with a highlighter and sticky notes can give you a different perspective on what you have found. If you have trouble visualizing the big picture of your project with a digital filing system, consider working with at least some of your research in hard copy as an alternative.

Researching Individual Types of Authority

Legal and Nonlegal Secondary Sources

A. INTRODUCTION ▼

As you read in Chapter 2, the term "primary authority" refers to a source of legal rules, such as a case, a statute, or an administrative regulation. Secondary authorities, by contrast, provide commentary on the law. Although they are not binding on courts and are not cited as frequently as primary sources, secondary sources are excellent research sources. Because they often summarize or collect authorities from a variety of jurisdictions, they can help you find binding or nonbinding primary authority on a subject. They also often provide narrative explanations of complex concepts that would be difficult to grasp thoroughly simply from reading primary authorities. Equipped with a solid understanding of the background of an area of law, you will be better able to locate and evaluate the primary authorities relevant to your research question.

1. When Secondary Sources Will Be Most Useful

Secondary sources will be most useful to you in the following situations:

▼ **When you are researching an area of law with which you are unfamiliar**
Secondary sources can give you the necessary background to generate search terms and understand a new area of law. They can also lead you directly to primary authorities.

▼ **When you are looking for nonbinding primary authority but do not know how to narrow the jurisdictions that are likely to have useful information**
If you need to find nonbinding primary authority on a subject, conducting a nationwide survey of the law on the topic is not likely to be an efficient research strategy. Secondary sources can help you locate nonbinding authorities relevant to your research question.

▼ **When you are researching an undeveloped area of the law**
When you are researching a question of first impression, commentators
may have discussed how the issue should be analyzed.

▼ **When an initial search for primary authorities yields either too**
  much or not enough information
If you are unable to find any useful information on a topic, you may
not be looking in the right places. Secondary sources can educate you
on the subject in a way that may allow you to expand or refocus your
research efforts. When your search yields an unmanageable amount of
information, secondary sources can do two things. First, their citations
to primary authorities can help you identify the most important authorities pertaining to the research question. Second, they can provide you
with information that may help you narrow your search or weed out
irrelevant sources.

2. Limits on the Appropriate Use of Secondary Sources

Knowing when not to use secondary sources is also important.
Secondary authorities are not binding. Therefore, you will not ordinarily
cite them in your written work. This is especially true if you use secondary sources to lead you to primary authorities. It is important never to
rely exclusively on a discussion of a primary authority that appears in a
secondary source. If you discuss a primary authority in a legal analysis,
you must read that authority yourself and update your research to make
sure it is current.

This is true for two reasons. First, a summary of a primary authority
might not include all of the information necessary to your analysis. It is
important to read the primary authority for yourself to make sure you
represent it correctly and thoroughly in your analysis.

Second, the information in the secondary source might not be completely current. Although most secondary sources are updated on
a regular basis, the law can change at any time. The source may contain incomplete information simply because of the inevitable time lag
between changes to the law and an update to the source. One mistake
some beginning researchers make is citing a secondary source for the text
of a case or statute without checking to make sure that the case has not
been overturned or that the statute has not been changed.

Another potential error is citing a secondary source for a proposition
about the state of the law generally, such as, "Forty-two states now rec-
ognize a cause of action for invasion of privacy based on disclosure of private facts." While a statement of that nature may well have been correct
when the secondary source was published, other states may have acted,
or some of those noted may have changed their law, in the intervening

time period. Accordingly, secondary sources should only be used as a starting point for locating primary authorities, not an ending point.

B. METHODS OF RESEARCHING LEGAL SECONDARY SOURCES ▼

If you can determine in your pre-search filtering which secondary sources are likely to contain useful information, your next step is locating relevant information within each source. Some legal secondary sources are only published in print. Few of the ones published online are available for free on the Internet. Therefore, you will use the search techniques described here most often either in print or in a commercial service such as Westlaw or Lexis. Both subject and word searching are common search techniques for secondary sources.

Print research is a good way to locate secondary sources by subject. Consequently, lawyers often prefer to research secondary sources in print even if they do other forms of research online. Not all law libraries maintain print collections of all of the secondary sources discussed in this chapter, so print research may not always be an option. Even if you conduct secondary source research online, however, you should be familiar with print research process. The citation rules for legal secondary sources flow from the print organization of the material and may make more sense to you if you understand how these sources are organized in print.

The print research process generally involves three steps: (1) using an index or table of contents to find references to material on the topic you are researching; (2) locating the material in the main text of the source; and (3) updating your research.

The first step is using an index or table of contents to find out where information on a topic is located within the secondary source. As with the index or table of contents in any other book, those in a secondary source will refer you to volumes, chapters, pages, or sections where you will find text explaining the topic you are researching. Some secondary sources consist of only a single volume. In those situations, you need simply to look up the index or table of contents references within the text. Often, however, the information in a secondary source is too comprehensive to fit within a single volume. In those cases, the source will consist of a multivolume set of books, which may be organized alphabetically by topic or numerically by volume number. The references in the index or table of contents will contain sufficient information for you to identify the appropriate book within the set, as well as the page or section number specifically relating to the topic you are researching. Locating material in the main text of the source is the second step in the process.

The final step in your research is updating the information you have located. Most print secondary sources are updated with pocket parts, as described in Chapter 6. The pocket part will be organized the same way as the main volume of the source. Thus, to update your research, you need to look up the same provisions in the pocket part that you read in the main text to find any additional information on the topic. If you do not find any reference to your topic in the pocket part, there is no new information to supplement the main text.

As you will see below, variations on this technique apply to some secondary sources. For the most part, however, you will be able to use this three-step process to research a variety of legal secondary sources in print.

When you conduct research online, you can use subject or word searching. If you identify secondary sources to research as part of your pre-search filtering, you can select the database for a specific secondary source when you get online. The database will often provide access to an index or table of contents you can use to search for information by subject. You can also execute a word search in the database for an individual secondary source.

If you do not identify specific secondary sources to research as part of your pre-search filtering, you can locate secondary sources through an unfiltered search in Westlaw, Lexis, Bloomberg Law, or another research service. The search results will include secondary sources, among other forms of authority. When you view the secondary sources your search retrieved, you can filter the results according to a number of criteria to focus on specific publications or types of content.

C. RESEARCHING COMMONLY USED LEGAL SECONDARY SOURCES ▼

This section describes the following commonly used legal secondary sources: legal encyclopedias, treatises, legal periodicals, *American Law Reports*, Restatements of the law, and uniform laws and model acts.

1. Legal Encyclopedias

Legal encyclopedias are just like the general subject encyclopedias you have used in other contexts, except they are limited in scope to legal subjects. Legal encyclopedias provide a general overview of the law on a variety of topics. They do not provide analysis or suggest solutions to conflicts in the law. Instead, they simply report on the general state of the law. Because encyclopedias cover the law in such a general way, you will usually use them to get background information on your research topic and, to a lesser extent, locate citations to primary authorities. You will rarely, if ever, cite a legal encyclopedia.

There are two general legal encyclopedias, *American Jurisprudence, Second Edition* (Am. Jur. 2d) and *Corpus Juris Secundum* (C.J.S.). In addition, encyclopedias are published for many individual states (e.g., *California Jurisprudence, Maryland Law Encyclopedia, Michigan Law and Practice*). When you are researching a question of state law, a state encyclopedia is often more helpful than a general encyclopedia for two reasons. First, the summary of the law will be tailored to the law of that state. Second, the citations to primary authorities will be from the controlling jurisdiction.

Because legal encyclopedias are published by commercial publishers, you can only access them in print or through a commercial service. As this text goes to press, only Westlaw and Lexis provide online access to Am. Jur. 2d and state encyclopedias. Westlaw also includes C.J.S. Other providers may add encyclopedias to their databases in the future.

You can research legal encyclopedias in print using the index-main volume-pocket part method described above. Online, you should be able to access the table of contents or execute a word search. The online version of an encyclopedia is updated periodically, not continuously, and may be only as current as the print version. Updates may not be incorporated into the main text until an updated print volume is published. Instead, updates appear in a separate section — sometimes labeled Supplement or Cumulative Supplement — that follows the main text of an entry. When you read an encyclopedia entry online, therefore, be sure to look for a separate section with updated information if it is available.

2. Treatises

Treatises have a narrower focus than legal encyclopedias. Where legal encyclopedias provide a general overview of a broad range of topics, treatises generally provide in-depth treatment of a single subject, such as torts or constitutional law. The goal of a treatise is to address in a systematic fashion all of the major topics within a subject area. Treatises often trace the history of the development of an area of law and explain the relationship of the treatise's subject to other areas of the law. To provide a comprehensive treatment of the subject's major topics, a treatise will explain the legal rules in the subject area, analyze major cases and statutes, and address policy issues underlying the rules. In addition to providing textual explanations, treatises also usually contain citations to many primary and secondary authorities.

Some treatises are widely respected and considered definitive sources in their subject areas. These treatises have often existed for a number of years and may be identified by the names of their original authors, even though other scholars now update and revise them. These well-known treatises can address broad areas of the law (Prosser on torts, Corbin on contracts, Wright & Miller on federal civil procedure) or more specialized subjects (Nimmer on copyright, White & Summers on the Uniform Commercial Code, Sutherland on statutory interpretation). These are not, however, the only treatises. Any book that provides comprehensive treatment of a single subject in a systematic fashion is a treatise, and many treatises exist on both broad areas of the law and narrower subjects. If you use a definitive treatise in your research, you might cite it in a brief or memorandum. Ordinarily, however, you will use treatises for research purposes and will not cite them in your written analysis.

Treatises are published by commercial publishers and are rarely accessible through a general Internet search. You will usually research treatises in print or through Westlaw, Lexis, Bloomberg Law, or another commercial provider. The holdings in different commercial services vary, so you may find a treatise in one service that is not available in others.

You can research treatises in print using the index-main volume-pocket part method described above. Online, you should be able to access the table of contents or execute a word search. The online version of a treatise is typically updated periodically, not continuously, and may be only as current as the print version. Updates may not be incorporated into the main text until an updated print volume is published. Instead, updates appear in a separate section that follows the main text of an entry. When you read a treatise online, therefore, be sure to look for a separate section with updated information if it is available.

3. Legal Periodicals

Articles in legal periodicals can be very useful research tools. You may hear periodical articles referred to as "law review" or "journal" articles. Many law schools publish periodicals known as law reviews or journals that collect articles on a wide range of topics. Many other types of legal periodicals also exist, however, including commercially published journals, legal newspapers, and magazines.

The commercial legal press includes magazines, such as the *ABA Journal* and local bar journals, and news sources such as *The National Law Journal.* These publications are good for keeping abreast of newsworthy developments in the law. Because they are news sources, their articles are generally short and focused more on describing legal developments than on analysis. These types of articles can provide limited background information, but they usually do not focus on the kinds of issues first-year law students research.

Articles published in law reviews or journals, by contrast, are thorough, thoughtful treatments of legal issues by law professors, judges, practitioners, and even students. The articles are usually focused fairly narrowly on specific issues, although they often include background or introductory sections that provide a general overview of the topic. They are generally well researched and contain citations to many primary and secondary authorities. In addition, they often address undeveloped areas in the law and propose solutions for resolving problems in the law. As a result, periodical articles can be useful for obtaining an overview of an area of law, finding references to primary and secondary authorities, and developing ideas for analyzing a question of first impression or resolving a conflict in the law.

Law review and journal articles fall into the following general categories:

▼ **Articles written by legal scholars**
These are articles written by law professors and other scholars. They frequently address problems or conflicts in the law. They may propose solutions to legal problems, advocate for changes to the law, identify new legal theories, or explore the relationship between the law and another discipline. Articles by leading or established scholars can be helpful in your research, especially if they explain doctrines or developments in a useful way. The weight of an individual article will depend on a number of factors, including the author's expertise, the reputation of the journal in which it is published, the article's age, and the depth of the article's research and analysis.

▼ **Articles written by judges and practitioners**
These are articles written by people who work with the law on a daily basis in very practical ways. Judges often write about their judicial philosophies or to offer advice or insights to practitioners. Practitioners may write about areas of law in which they practice. These articles may help you understand a legal issue and provide an overview of important authorities, but practitioner articles in particular may not have the depth of other types of articles.

▼ **Student notes and comments**
These are articles written by law students. Often, they describe a significant new case or statute. They may analyze a problem in the law and propose a solution. Because these articles are written by students, they carry less weight than other periodical articles and are useful primarily for background information and citations to primary authorities.

These are, of course, generalizations that may not hold true in every instance. For the most part, however, you will use law review and journal articles to deepen your understanding of an issue, rather than as support for written analysis. You will not ordinarily cite an article if you can support your analysis with primary authorities. If you cannot find primary support, however, you might cite a persuasive article. Additionally, if you incorporate an argument or analysis from an article in your written work, it is important to cite the source to avoid plagiarism.

Periodical articles are unique among legal authorities in that there is no way to update an individual article short of locating later articles that add to or criticize an earlier article. As a consequence, it is important to note the date of any periodical article you use. If the article is more than a few years old, you might want to supplement your research with more current material. In addition, if you use the article to lead you to primary authorities, you will need to update your research using the updating tools available for those authorities to make sure your research is completely current.

Westlaw and Lexis provide access to many legal periodical articles dating to the 1980s. Bloomberg Law also contains legal periodicals, although the dates of coverage vary by publication. In any of these services, you can search a database of legal periodicals, and periodical articles are included with the results of an unfiltered search. Unlike other legal secondary sources, however, legal periodicals are also available from many other information providers.

One way to locate legal periodical articles is through a periodical index. Two commonly used periodical indexes are the Index to Legal Periodicals (ILP) and LegalTrac. These services index a wide range of periodicals and provide full text access to many articles. ILP and LegalTrac are subscription services. You should be able to access either or both through your law library's research portal.

HeinOnline is another service that provides online access to legal periodicals, among other types of authority. It is also a subscription service accessible through your law library's research portal. HeinOnline's holdings go back further in time than those of Westlaw, Lexis, and Bloomberg Law, often dating back to the inception of the periodicals in its database. You can retrieve an article from its citation, search by title or author, or conduct word searches in the full text of the articles in HeinOnline's database. You can also browse the table of contents of individual publications. HeinOnline displays articles in.pdf format.

A significant amount of recent legal scholarship in law reviews and journals is available online free of charge through the Social Science Research Network (SSRN) and Digital Commons. SSRN provides access to scholarly articles in a number of fields, including law. Authors make their published work and ongoing research available by posting it on SSRN. Because SSRN relies on authors to post their own work, its coverage is somewhat idiosyncratic, but many legal academics have posted their entire publishing histories. Digital Commons is another source for access to law review articles, as well as scholarship in other fields. Digital Commons hosts repositories where institutions post online versions of their publications. Some reproduce the print version in an online format, some offer online supplements to their traditional publications, and some publish exclusively online through their institutional repositories.

You can locate legal periodical articles using a general Internet search. Google Scholar, a specialty version of Google's search engine, allows you to search for law journal articles. Sometimes, however, access to the full text requires a subscription to the service (such as HeinOnline) that hosts the article.

You can also access law review or journal articles by going directly to the publication's website. Most schools post their current volume, at least some of their prior volumes, and any online supplements to the main publication. If you have the citation to an article, this can be a quick and economical way to obtain it.

4. *American Law Reports*

American Law Reports, or A.L.R., contains articles called Annotations. Annotations collect summaries of cases from a variety of jurisdictions to provide an overview of the law on a topic. The publisher describes annotations as research briefs summarizing case law and providing objective analysis of both sides of specific legal issues.[1] Because A.L.R. Annotations provide summaries of individual cases, they are more detailed than encyclopedia entries, but because they address specific legal topics, you will not always find one relevant to your research issue.

A.L.R. Annotations are especially helpful at the beginning of your research to give you an overview of a topic. Because Annotations collect summaries of cases from many jurisdictions, they can also be helpful in directing you toward binding or nonbinding primary authorities. More recent Annotations also contain references to other research sources, such as other secondary sources and tools for conducting additional case research. Although A.L.R. is a useful research tool, you will rarely, if ever, cite an A.L.R. Annotation.

There are multiple series of A.L.R. that proceed in chronological order. A.L.R. first through seventh series address issues of state law, although they bring in federal law as appropriate to the topic. A.L.R. Federal consists of three series that are devoted to issues of federal law. Each series contains multiple volumes organized by volume number. A.L.R. International addresses international law issues.

A.L.R. is a ThomsonReuters (West) publication that you can access only in print or through a commercial service. All of the A.L.R. series are available in Westlaw; all but the first and international series are available in Lexis. In the future, other providers may add A.L.R. to their databases.

---

1. ThomsonReuters Legal, *American Law Reports*, https://legal.thomsonreuters.com/en/products/westlaw/american-law-reports (last visited September 16, 2019).

If you research A.L.R. in print, you can use the index-main volume-pocket part process described above. A.L.R. publishes a single set of index volumes for all A.L.R. series except the first one. A.L.R. also publishes a digest, which is a research tool described in Chapter 9. You do not have to use the digest to locate A.L.R. Annotations, however, because the index will direct you to relevant information.

The online version of an A.L.R. Annotation is typically only as current as the print version. Updates from the pocket part are not incorporated into the text. Material from the print pocket part appears as a separate portion of text following the main text of each section. When you read an A.L.R. Annotation online, therefore, be sure to look for updated information if it is available.

5. Restatements

The American Law Institute publishes what are called Restatements of the law in a variety of fields. You may already be familiar with the Restatements for contracts or torts from your other classes. Restatements essentially restate the common-law rules on a subject. Restatements have been published in the following fields:

- Agency
- Conflicts of Laws
- Contracts
- Foreign Relations Law of the United States
- Judgments
- Property
- Restitution
- Security
- Suretyship and Guaranty
- The Law Governing Lawyers
- Torts
- Trusts
- Unfair Competition

In determining what the common-law rules are, the Restatements often look to the rules in the majority of U.S. jurisdictions. Sometimes, however, the Restatements will also state emerging rules where the rules seem to be changing or propose rules in areas where the authors believe a change in the law would be appropriate. Although the Restatements are limited to common-law doctrines, the rules in the Restatements are set out almost like statutes, with individual sections containing legal rules. In addition to setting out the common-law rules for a subject, the Restatements also provide commentary on the proper interpretations of the rules, illustrations demonstrating how the rules should apply in certain situations, and summaries of cases applying and interpreting the Restatement.

Although a Restatement is a secondary source, it is one with substantial weight. A court can adopt a Restatement's view of an issue, which then makes the comments and illustrations especially persuasive in that jurisdiction. If you are researching the law of a jurisdiction that has adopted a Restatement, you can use the Restatement effectively to locate nonbinding authority from other Restatement jurisdictions. As a result, a Restatement is an especially valuable secondary source.

A print Restatement consists of two components: the Restatement rules volumes, which contain the Restatement rules, comments, and illustrations; and the Appendix volumes, which contain case summaries. To research a Restatement in print, you must follow two steps: (1) find relevant sections of the Restatement in the rules volumes; and (2) find case summaries interpreting the Restatement in the Appendix volumes.

In print, the subject index or table of contents in the Restatement rules volumes will direct you to individual sections of the Restatement. In the second step, you need to go to the separate Appendix volumes. The Appendix volumes are organized numerically by Restatement section number. By looking up the appropriate section number, you will find cases from a variety of jurisdictions interpreting that section. The Appendix volumes are not cumulative. Each volume covers only a specific period of time. Therefore, to find all of the cases interpreting a section, you would need to look it up in each Appendix volume. The latest Appendix volume will have a pocket part with the most recent references.

Because Restatements are published by a commercial publisher, they are not consistently available on the Internet. You can find selected sections of Restatements with a general Internet search engine or through free research services, but you will not always find complete compilations of these sources, nor will you find the comments, illustrations, or annotations. More often, you will research Restatements in print or with a commercial service such as Westlaw, Lexis, or Bloomberg Law.

When you research a Restatement in Westlaw, be aware that the Restatement rules, comments, illustrations, and case summaries are compiled together. Therefore, when you retrieve a section of a Restatement, you will see all of these items together in a single document. You can browse a Restatement's table of contents or execute a word search to locate useful information. If you execute an unfiltered search in Westlaw, Restatement references will be included in the section with other secondary sources.

Lexis separates Restatement rules from the case summaries. You can execute word searches or browse the table of contents in a rules database. When you retrieve a rule section from a Restatement, you will see the rule, comments, and illustrations together in a single document. Case summaries, however, are separated from the rules. The About this Document section to the right of the rule text contains a link to Citators, which retrieves summaries of cases that have cited the Restatement section.

If you execute an unfiltered search in Lexis, Restatement rule references will be included in the section with other secondary sources.

Bloomberg Law provides access to some, but not all, Restatements. It organizes Restatements the same way the print sets are organized. Rules are separated from case summaries. You can select a Restatement's rules, Appendix, or both as sources to search under U.S. Secondary Sources. Restatements are categorized by content type under Books and Treatises and then under a subcategory for the American Law Institute (ALI). If you execute an unfiltered search, Restatements are included, but entries from the rules volumes will be listed separately from those from the appendix volumes in the search results.

6. Uniform Laws and Model Acts

Uniform laws and model acts are proposed statutes that can be enacted by legislatures. Two examples you may already know about are the Uniform Commercial Code (UCC) and the Model Penal Code. Uniform laws and model acts are similar to Restatements in that they set out proposed rules, followed by commentary, research notes, and summaries of cases interpreting the rules. Unlike Restatements, which are limited to common-law doctrines, uniform laws and model acts exist in areas governed by statutory law.

Although uniform laws and model acts look like statutes, they are secondary sources. Their provisions do not take on the force of law unless they are enacted by a legislature. When that happens, however, the commentary, research references, and case summaries become very useful research tools. They can help you interpret the statute and direct you to nonbinding authority from other jurisdictions that have enacted the statute.

You are most likely to research uniform laws and model acts when your project involves research into state statutes. In print, a multivolume set called *Uniform Laws Annotated* (ULA) contains the text of uniform laws along with commentary and summaries of cases that have interpreted the uniform laws. The ULA set has its own finding tools that are explained in a booklet called the *Directory of Uniform Acts and Codes: Tables–Index*. You should review this booklet for guidance in using this source.

You can find some uniform laws or model acts with a general Internet search or through free research services. But you will not always find complete compilations of these sources, nor will you find the comments, research notes, or case summaries. To research uniform laws in Westlaw, Lexis, or Bloomberg Law, you can select an appropriate database and then either execute a word search or view a statute's table of contents. These three services draw from different sources, so although the text of a uniform law will be the same in each, the research references associated with the uniform laws may vary. Unfiltered searches in Lexis include information on model acts and uniform laws under statutes and legislation. Bloomberg Law also includes references to uniform laws in the results of an unfiltered search under legislative materials. Use the option to See All content types to narrow the results to uniform laws.

D. RESEARCHING NONLEGAL SECONDARY SOURCES ___▼

Legal research used to be accomplished primarily, if not exclusively, in a limited universe of research sources produced by legal publishers. The secondary sources discussed so far in this chapter are the traditional sources used for legal research, but many nontraditional secondary sources are now available on the Internet.

Government, educational, nonprofit, trade, and civic organizations that are engaged in public education efforts make useful information on many areas of the law available via their websites. Sources such as Wikipedia contain information about the law. Free legal research sites like FindLaw often include articles written by lawyers or legal commentators. A general search engine like Google can lead to useful secondary information about the law. In addition, blogs are becoming an increasingly important source of information both in our culture as a whole and in legal research. Law-related blogs are sometimes called blawgs.

These nontraditional sources are secondary sources, and all of the caveats regarding appropriate uses of traditional legal secondary sources apply to them with equal force. Lawyers do not consider these sources authoritative, and it is difficult to imagine circumstances under which you would cite one.

Using publicly available Internet sites can be both easier and harder than using more traditional legal research tools. It can be easier in the sense that Internet sources are cost-effective to use and can provide easy access to information relevant to your research. It can be harder in the sense that you cannot assume that a nontraditional secondary source is reliable. It is important to remember that any person with a message can publish material on the Internet. And because online sources can be updated at any time, they may be perceived as providing current information even if they have not been updated for a long period of time. Therefore, you must take special care to evaluate any secondary information you find on the Internet.

Publicly available Internet sources are most likely to be useful to you when you are looking for information on a specific topic. If you find a relevant website or blog, it may provide you with background information on the topic, references to significant legal authorities, news about legislative initiatives pending at the local, state, or federal level, and links to other sites with useful information.

To make sure you use publicly available Internet sources appropriately, you should follow four steps: (1) locate useful information; (2) assess the credibility of the source of the information; (3) save or print a copy of the information you are using; and (4) verify and update any primary authorities you locate through the source.

To locate useful information, you could use a general search engine, such as Google, or a specialized search engine, such as Google Scholar for scholarly publications or LawCrawler (the search engine in FindLaw) for law-related websites. You can also use a directory such as Blawg, a directory of law-related blogs.

Once you have located useful information, you must assess the credibility of the source. Many individuals and groups post information on the Internet to advance their social or policy agendas. Therefore, you need to make a separate assessment of how much weight to give to information posted on an individual's or organization's website. The sites you visit should contain information you can use to assess the sources' credibility. Most sites sponsored by organizations or entities include information about the group, such as its history and mission. The authors of many blogs will provide biographical information to help you assess their expertise.

If you find useful information on the Internet, be sure to save or print a copy of the page. Internet sites can change at any moment; the information most helpful to you could change or disappear altogether at any time. If you find that information you accessed earlier is no longer available, you can try to find it in an Internet archive, such as the Internet Archive Wayback Machine, which stores copies of sites for future reference. The University of North Texas library system also hosts the CyberCemetery of Former Federal Websites. Although these sites provide limited historical records of Internet sites, you cannot count on finding an archived version of a web page that has been changed, moved, or deleted. The better practice, therefore, is to save or print useful information as you locate it.

If you find references to primary authorities through publicly available websites, the last step is verifying and updating your research. You should not assume that the authorities you have located are correct, complete, or up to date. Use the information you have found as a springboard into more traditional avenues of legal research to make sure that you have located all pertinent information and that everything you cite is authoritative.

Cases

A. INTRODUCTION ▼

1. The Structure of the Court System

The United States has more than 50 separate court systems, including the federal system, the 50 state systems, and the District of Columbia system. You may recall from Chapter 2 that the federal system has three levels of courts: U.S. District Courts (the trial courts), U.S. Courts of Appeals (the intermediate appellate courts), and the U.S. Supreme Court (the court of last resort). Most state court systems are structured similarly to the federal court system.

Judges from any of these courts can issue written decisions, and their decisions are one source of legal rules. This chapter focuses on where these decisions are published and how you can locate them.

2. Sources of Cases

When a court issues a written decision, the decision is a public document filed with the clerk of the court and is called a slip opinion. Written opinions are collected together and published in chronological order in print. The books containing cases are called reporters. Although most cases are also available online, they are still largely organized and cited according to the print reporter system. Additionally, you can tell much about the authoritative value of a case from its citation if you understand the print reporter system. Therefore, you need to be familiar with print reporters.

Many sets of reporters are limited to opinions from a single jurisdiction or level of court. Thus, for example, federal reporters contain opinions from federal courts, and state reporters contain opinions from state courts. In addition, each set of reporters may be subdivided into different series covering different time periods.

A reporter published under government authority is known as an official reporter. Reporters published by commercial publishers are called unofficial reporters. Because these two types of reporters exist, the same opinion may be published in more than one reporter. The text of the opinion should be exactly the same in an official and an unofficial reporter; the only difference is that the former is published by the government, and the latter is not. When a case appears in more than one reporter, it is described as having parallel citations. This is because each set of reporters will have its own citation for the case.

The only federal cases published by the government are those of the U.S. Supreme Court; these are published in a reporter called *United States Reports*. State governments usually publish the decisions of their highest courts, and most also publish cases from some of their lower courts.

Perhaps the largest commercial publisher of cases is Thomson Reuters/West, formerly West Publishing Company. West has created a network of unofficial reporters called the National Reporter System, which comprises reporters with decisions from almost every U.S. jurisdiction. West publishes U.S. Supreme Court decisions in the *Supreme Court Reporter*. Decisions from the U.S. Courts of Appeals are published in the *Federal Reporter*, and those from U.S. District Courts are published in the *Federal Supplement*. West also publishes some specialized reporters that contain decisions from the federal courts. For example, *Federal Rules Decisions* (F.R.D.) contains federal district court decisions interpreting the Federal Rules of Civil and Criminal Procedure, and the *Federal Appendix* (F. App'x) contains nonprecedential opinions from the federal courts of appeals. (Nonprecedential opinions are discussed in more detail below.) West publishes state cases in what are called regional reporters. West has divided the country into seven regions. The reporter for each region collects state cases from each state within that region.

Figure 9.1 shows where cases from the various state and federal courts can be found. Cases from most states can be found in the state's official reporter, as well as in the reporters listed in Figure 9.1.

Almost all cases are identified by West reporter citations, official reporter citations, or both, and you can obtain a case from either of these types of print reporters. But you can obtain cases from other sources as well. Virtually any online commercial service, including Westlaw, Lexis, Bloomberg Law, Casemaker, Fastcase, and others, will give you access to cases. Cases are also largely publicly available online. Free online sources include the deciding court's website, FindLaw, and Cornell Law School's Legal Information Institute, among others. Although you can find cases using Google, a better option for case research is Google Scholar, a specialized search engine that allows you to search specifically for case law. Some of these sources have more comprehensive coverage than others, so you should check that the source you use provides access to cases from the appropriate jurisdiction and time period for your research.

▼ FIGURE 9.1   Reporters

COURT or JURISDICTION	REPORTER (followed by reporter abbreviation; multiple abbreviations denote multiple series)
United States Supreme Court	*United States Reports* (U.S.)* *Supreme Court Reporter* (S. Ct.) *United States Supreme Court Reports, Lawyer's Edition* (L. Ed., L. Ed. 2d)
United States Courts of Appeals	*Federal Reporter* (F., F.2d, F.3d) *Federal Appendix* (F. App'x)
United States District Courts	*Federal Supplement* (F. Supp., F. Supp. 2d, F. Supp. 3d) *Federal Rules Decisions* (F.R.D.)
Atlantic Region states (Connecticut, Delaware, District of Columbia, Maine, Maryland, New Hampshire, New Jersey, Pennsylvania, Rhode Island, Vermont)	*Atlantic Reporter* (A., A.2d, A.3d)
North Eastern Region states (Illinois, Indiana, Massachusetts, New York, Ohio)	*North Eastern Reporter* (N.E., N.E.2d, N.E.3d) New York: *New York Supplement* (N.Y.S., N.Y.S.2d, N.Y.S.3d) Illinois: *Illinois Decisions* (Ill. Dec.)
South Eastern Region states (Georgia, North Carolina, South Carolina, Virginia, West Virginia)	*South Eastern Reporter* (S.E., S.E.2d)
Southern Region states (Alabama, Florida, Louisiana, Mississippi)	*Southern Reporter* (So., So. 2d, So. 3d)
South Western Region states (Arkansas, Kentucky, Missouri, Tennessee, Texas)	*South Western Reporter* (S.W., S.W.2d, S.W.3d)
North Western Region states (Iowa, Michigan, Minnesota, Nebraska, North Dakota, South Dakota, Wisconsin)	*North Western Reporter* (N.W., N.W.2d, N.W.3d)
Pacific Region states (Alaska, Arizona, California, Colorado, Hawaii, Idaho, Kansas, Montana, Nevada, New Mexico, Oklahoma, Oregon, Utah, Washington, Wyoming)	*Pacific Reporter* (P., P.2d, P.3d) California: *California Reporter* (Cal. Rptr., Cal. Rptr. 2d, Cal. Rptr. 3d)

* Official reporter published by the federal government.

3. The Anatomy of a Published Case

A published case begins with a heading containing the parties' names, the court that rendered the decision, and the date of the decision. If the case has parallel citations, the heading may also include the citations to the other reporters where the case is published. After the heading, you will see the names of the attorneys who represented the parties and the judge or judges who decided the case. The opinion of the court follows these preliminary items. If the decision has any concurring or dissenting opinions, they will follow immediately after the majority or plurality opinion.

Published cases often include editorial enhancements to help you with your research. These enhancements include a synopsis of the case and one or more paragraphs summarizing the key points in the case. These summary paragraphs are called headnotes. Headnotes allow you to research cases by subject, as explained more fully below.

Editorial enhancements that accompany a case are written by case editors, not by the court. Although they are useful for research, anything that is not part of the court's opinion does not constitute primary authority. In a few jurisdictions, the court adds its own summary or syllabus that contains the holding of the case. Unless you see a notation indicating otherwise, however, you should treat only the text of the court's opinion as authoritative.

If a case is available both in a print reporter and online, the online version usually includes page numbers from the print version placed in brackets, marked by stars, or both. Thus, the online version would include a notation like [123], *123, or [*123] to indicate where page 123 of the print version begins. You need the print page numbers for a proper citation to the case. Pagination for parallel citations may or may not be included.

Many appellate courts post their slip opinions online as soon as cases are decided. Because a slip opinion is issued before the case appears in a reporter, these opinions look like ordinary typed documents. They typically do not include any editorial enhancements and are identified by case number or party names instead of by reporter citation.

After the court issues a slip opinion, the case may be published in print in an official reporter, an unofficial reporter, or both. If the case is published in print in an official reporter, a synopsis or headnotes may be added. Commercial publishers of unofficial reporters typically add editorial enhancements to cases, but Google Scholar and other free services do not.

A case published in a West print reporter and in Westlaw includes a synopsis and headnotes. The headnotes are unique to West and are different from headnotes created by other publishers. For cases with parallel citations, Westlaw includes pagination for multiple reporters.

A published case in Lexis includes a synopsis and LexisNexis Headnotes. These headnotes are unique to Lexis and are different from headnotes created by other publishers. For cases with parallel citations, Lexis includes pagination for multiple reporters.

Bloomberg Law does not add its own synopsis to a case. It identifies relevant text within a case with a feature called Points of Law. You can identify specific subjects an opinion discusses by selecting Points of Law and browsing the document. Additionally, cases in some subject areas have headnotes called BNA Headnotes. Bloomberg Law acquired the holdings of another publisher, the Bureau of National Affairs (BNA), which had its own case reporters and headnote system. Cases in the subject areas covered by the BNA reporters have BNA Headnotes. BNA Headnotes are unique to Bloomberg Law and are different from headnotes created by other publishers. Bloomberg Law provides pagination for multiple reporters for some cases, but not all.

4. Unpublished, or Nonprecedential, Opinions

Not all cases are published; only those designated by the courts for publication appear in print reporters. The opinions not designated for publication are called unpublished opinions. In the past, the only ways to obtain copies of unpublished opinions were from the parties to the case or from the clerk's office at the courthouse. This is still true today for some unpublished opinions, especially those issued by state courts. Many unpublished opinions, however, are available online. The federal courts of appeals make many of their unpublished opinions available on their websites. In addition, unpublished opinions issued by the federal courts of appeals since 2001 are available in print in the *Federal Appendix*, a West reporter.

Because these opinions are increasingly available both online and in print, the term "unpublished" opinion has become a misnomer. A more accurate term is "nonprecedential" opinion. Nonprecedential opinions are often subject to special court rules. For example, unlike cases published in the *Federal Reporter*, those appearing in the *Federal Appendix* are not treated as binding precedent by the courts, which is why they are described as nonprecedential opinions. In the past, the federal courts of appeals often limited the circumstances under which nonprecedential opinions could be cited in documents filed with the court. Federal nonprecedential opinions issued on or after January 1, 2007, may now be cited without restriction. Because of restrictions on citations to earlier nonprecedential opinions, many cases in the *Federal Appendix* contain notations indicating that they are not binding precedent and cautioning readers to check court rules before citing them. Nonprecedential opinions by other courts may also be subject to special rules.

Although courts have issued nonprecedential opinions for many years, the practice is not without controversy. The authoritative value of nonprecedential opinions is a subject of ongoing debate in the legal community. Regardless of the controversy, nonprecedential opinions can be valuable research tools. Therefore, you should not disregard them when you are conducting case research.

B. METHODS OF RESEARCHING CASES ⎯⎯⎯⎯⎯⎯⎯▼

As noted above, cases are available from many sources. If you have the citation to a case that you have obtained from another source, such as a secondary source, you can easily locate the case in print or online.

When you do not have a citation, you can locate cases by subject, by words in the document, or by party name. If your pre-search filtering indicates that you should research cases from a specific jurisdiction, limiting your search to that jurisdiction's cases will make it easier for you to evaluate your search results.

Researching by subject is often a useful way to locate cases. Reviewing summaries of cases arranged by subject can help you identify those that address the topic of your research. You can search by subject in print using a research tool called a digest, which is explained more fully below. Some online services provide access to a digest or allow you to search for cases using subject categories. Word searching is another way to locate cases online.

One additional search option is locating a case by party name. In print, you can use a directory of cases organized by party name. Online, you can use a party name as a term in a word search; many services also have search templates that allow you to enter party names.

If you execute an unfiltered search in Westlaw, Lexis, or Bloomberg Law, your search results will include cases. You will ordinarily pre-filter your search by jurisdiction unless you are researching the law of all U.S. jurisdictions. When you review the cases your search has retrieved, you can filter the results according to a number of criteria, such as cases from a particular level of court.

C. TOOLS FOR ONLINE CASE RESEARCH ⎯⎯⎯⎯⎯⎯⎯▼

1. Researching Cases by Subject with an Online Digest

Reporters are published in chronological order; they are not organized by subject. Trying to research cases in chronological order would be impossible. A digest is a research tool that organizes cases by subject. You can use a digest to locate cases by topic.

The term "digest" literally means to arrange and summarize, and that is exactly what a digest does. In a digest, the law is arranged into different subject categories, such as torts, contracts, or criminal law. Then, within each category, the digest provides summaries of cases that discuss the law on that subject. You can use the summaries to decide which cases you should read to find the answer to your research question.

The West digest system is well respected in legal research. West has divided the law into more than 400 subject categories, called topics. The West topics are quite broad. Subject areas such as torts or contracts generate thousands of cases. Therefore, the topics have been further subdivided into smaller categories. Each subdivision within a topic is assigned a number that West calls a key number.

West assigns a topic and key number to each headnote at the beginning of a case. It then collects the headnotes and arranges them by topic and key number. Thus, under each topic and key number, the case summary you find in a West digest will correspond exactly to one of the headnotes at the beginning of a case published in a West reporter. By reviewing summaries organized by topic and key number, you can locate cases on a specific subject.

West case summaries, topics, and key numbers can only be accessed through Westlaw or West print digests (described in Section D, below). Other publishers have their own headnote and digesting systems that are organized similarly to the West digest system.

You can access the West digest case summaries in Westlaw in two ways. One way is from a case on point. The headnotes at the beginning of each case summarize the content of the case and have topics and key numbers assigned to them. By following the links in the headnotes, you can retrieve summaries of additional cases that have been assigned the same topic and key number.

The second way to access the West digest is to search through the digest topic headings. You can access the directory of topics from the All Content tab using the Key Numbers link. You can expand the topics listed to see specific key numbers.

You can research cases by subject in Lexis in much the same way. Use the links to the subject headings above each headnote or the More Like This Headnote link following each headnote to search for additional authority by subject.

Bloomberg Law also allows you to search by subject. With Points of Law, clicking on highlighted text brings up a list of cases on the same topic. For cases with BNA Headnotes, a topic number (called a Classification Number) appears after the headnote. Click on the Classification Number to find additional cases.

One of the most difficult aspects of digest research is deciding which cases to read based on the summaries. If you are reviewing digest summaries that include cases from more than one jurisdiction, you might want to filter the display to those from the controlling jurisdiction. Otherwise, paying attention to the citations will help you stay focused on the summaries of cases from the appropriate jurisdiction. In addition, many case summaries include not only a synopsis of the rule the court applied in the case, but also a concise description of the facts. You can use the factual summaries to narrow down the cases applicable to your research question.

Even a fact-specific summary, however, does not provide the full context of the case. Using the digest is only the first step in researching cases; all the digest can do is point you toward cases that may help answer your research question. Digest summaries, like headnotes, are editorial enhancements designed to assist you with your research. They are not authoritative, and you should never rely on one as a statement of the law. Always read the case in full before relying on it to answer a research question.

2. Tools for Evaluating and Expanding Case Research Search Results

Citation, subject, and word searching are established methods for conducting research. Once you have obtained search results, you can use tools specifically intended to help you evaluate and expand the results. You are not likely to use these tools in your initial efforts to research case law. Once you have begun to define the contours of a research question governed by case law, however, you may find them useful.

Research results are typically presented in list form. With case research, a search retrieves a list of citations and case summaries. You usually have some ability to alter the list order. For example, you may be able to list the "most cited" cases first. But a list of authorities will not necessarily make the most significant cases on your research question apparent.

Viewing results using a visual map may make it easier for you to evaluate the strength or relative importance of authorities. It may also allow you to trace the development of a doctrine. Three research tools that present information visually are Ravel, Fastcase, and SCOTUS Mapper.

Ravel is owned by Lexis, so you can use the search visualization function in Ravel or with the Ravel View feature in Lexis. The visualization function in Fastcase is called the Interactive Timeline. Search visualization functions present search results in map form. Each opinion within the results is represented by a circle on a grid. The size of the circle is meant to represent the relative importance of the case; the more the case has been cited, the larger the circle. Placing your cursor over the circle reveals information about the case, such as its name and citation This type of visual mapping can make it easier to identify key cases and focus your research.

When you use a visual map, do not uncritically select cases based on the circle size. Depending on the scope of your search, the grid may include cases from outside the controlling jurisdiction. You would ordinarily prefer a binding case to a nonbinding case, even one that has been cited frequently. Also, a new case may have a small circle simply because it is new and has not been cited as frequently as older cases. But if the new case changes, extends, or adds to the law on your research issue, it may be more important than the size of the circle would indicate. The visual map is a tool you can use to evaluate case law search results, but you still need to make your own judgments about the usefulness of the authorities.

SCOTUS Mapper is a tool for creating visual maps showing lines of authority in the U.S. Supreme Court's development of legal doctrines. The tool allows users to create their own maps; additionally, maps for many areas of Supreme Court doctrine already exist in the SCOTUS Mapping Project's libraries. Links within the existing maps retrieve the full text of the cases. The mapping tool focuses on decisions of the U.S. Supreme Court, making it most useful for researching federal constitutional and statutory issues. It may eventually become available for cases from other courts.

Another type of search tool analyzes a written document to retrieve relevant case law. Quick Check in Westlaw and CARA (Case Analysis Research Assistant) in Casetext are document analysis tools. Lexis is introducing a brief analysis tool as well. With document analysis tools, you upload a document, such as a brief, and the tool analyzes the text, citations, and other information in the document to generate research recommendations. These tools are unique because they do not require you to execute a query to retrieve search results. Instead, they use the content in the document itself to generate the results.

Document analysis tools are, in a sense, hybrid tools that combine aspects of a search engine with the functions of a citator. (A citator is a tool that allows you to determine whether a case has been cited elsewhere, and if so, how it has been treated. Citators are discussed in detail in Chapter 10.)

As a beginning researcher, you may find the tools described here most useful for refining initial search results obtained through traditional research methods. But they represent potential new directions for research methodology and may become go-to resources in the future.

D. PRINT RESEARCH WITH WEST DIGESTS ⎯⎯⎯⎯⎯⎯▼

If you are conducting case research in print, you will almost certainly use a digest to locate cases on your topic. The West digest system, described in Section C, above, is the best known print digest system. The integrated system of topics, key numbers, and case headnotes is the same in print as it is in Westlaw. You will typically follow four steps to research cases with West print digests:

1. locating the correct digest set for the type of research you are doing;
2. locating relevant topics and key numbers within the digest;
3. reading the case summaries under the topics and key numbers;
4. updating your research to make sure you find summaries of the most recent cases.

1. Locating the Correct Digest Set

Reporters and digests are similar in several ways. Just as there are different reporters containing cases from different jurisdictions, there are also different sets of digests for finding cases from these various jurisdictions. And just as a case can be published in more than one reporter, a case can also be summarized in more than one digest. Thus, the first step in finding cases that will help you answer a research question is choosing the correct digest set.

Digest sets are organized by jurisdiction and by date. The four jurisdictional categories for digests are federal, state, regional, and combined. A federal digest, as you might imagine, summarizes federal cases. A state digest contains summaries of cases from that state as well as those from the federal courts located in that state. A regional digest summarizes state cases from the states within the region, but it does not contain summaries of any federal cases. West publishes regional digests for some, but not all, of its regional reporters. A combined digest summarizes cases from all state and federal jurisdictions.

Within each category, the digest set may be divided into different series covering different time periods. For example, the coverage of *West's Federal Practice Digest*, Fifth Series begins in 2003. Earlier cases, from the early 1980s to 2003, can be found in the Fourth Series. Ordinarily, you will want to begin your research in the most current series. If you are unable to find information in the most current series, however, you could locate older cases by looking in the earlier series.

Figures 9.2 through 9.4 summarize some of the characteristics of West digests.

To decide which digest is the best choice for your research, you will need to consider the nature and scope of the project. Usually, you will want to choose the narrowest digest that still has enough information for you to find relevant cases. Sometimes you will need to use more than one digest to find all of the cases you need.

▼ FIGURE 9.2   Federal Digests

DESCRIPTION	*WEST'S FEDERAL PRACTICE DIGEST, FIFTH SERIES*	*WEST'S UNITED STATES SUPREME COURT DIGEST*
What is included	Summaries of cases from all federal courts	Summaries of U.S. Supreme Court cases
What is excluded	Summaries of state cases	Summaries of cases from lower federal courts and all state courts
Coverage	Summaries of cases from 2003 to present appear in the Fifth Series. Older cases are summarized in prior series of this set (e.g., *West's Federal Practice Digest,* Fourth Series).	Summaries of all U.S. Supreme Court cases

▼ FIGURE 9.3   State and Regional Digests

DESCRIPTION	STATE DIGESTS	REGIONAL DIGESTS
What is included	Summaries of cases from the state's courts and the federal courts within the state	Summaries of cases from the state courts within the region
What is excluded	Summaries of state and federal cases from courts outside the state	Summaries of state cases from states outside the region and all federal cases
Coverage	West publishes state digests for all states except Delaware, Nevada, and Utah. The *Virginia and West Virginia Digest* summarizes cases from both of those states. The *Dakota Digest* summarizes cases from both North and South Dakota. Some state digests have multiple series.	West publishes Atlantic, North Western, Pacific, and South Eastern Digests. West *does not* publish North Eastern, Southern, or South Western Digests. All of the regional digests have multiple series.

▼ FIGURE 9.4   Combined Digests

DESCRIPTION	COMBINED DIGESTS
What is included	Summaries of state and federal cases from all jurisdictions across the United States
What is excluded	Nothing
Coverage	The combined digests are divided into the *Decennial* and *Century Digests,* covering the following dates:

Twelfth Decennial Digest, Part 4	2017-2019
Twelfth Decennial Digest, Part 3	2013-2016
Twelfth Decennial Digest, Part 2	2010-2013
Twelfth Decennial Digest, Part 1	2008-2010
Eleventh Decennial Digest, Part 3	2004-2007
Eleventh Decennial Digest, Part 2	2001-2004
Eleventh Decennial Digest, Part 1	1996-2001
Tenth Decennial Digest, Part 2	1991-1996
Tenth Decennial Digest, Part 1	1986-1991
Ninth Decennial Digest, Part 2	1981-1986
Ninth Decennial Digest, Part 1	1976-1981
Eighth Decennial Digest	1966-1976
Seventh Decennial Digest	1956-1966
Sixth Decennial Digest	1946-1956
Fifth Decennial Digest	1936-1946
Fourth Decennial Digest	1926-1936
Third Decennial Digest	1916-1926
Second Decennial Digest	1907-1916
First Decennial Digest	1897-1906
Century Digest	1658-1896

West's Federal Practice Digest is the best place to start looking for federal cases. If you are researching case law from an individual state, the digest from that state is usually the best starting place. If you do not have access to the state digest, the regional digest is another good place to look. It is also a good place to find persuasive authority from surrounding jurisdictions. Remember, however, that regional digests summarize only state cases, not federal cases. Therefore, if you also want to find cases from the federal courts located within an individual state, you will need to supplement your regional digest research by using *West's Federal Practice Digest.*

The combined digests have the most comprehensive coverage, but they are also the most difficult to use. You would probably begin with the *Twelfth Decennial Digest* and then consult as many previous series as necessary to locate cases on your topic. Because this is a cumbersome process, the combined digests are usually only useful when you know the approximate time period you want to research or when you are conducting nationwide research.

Figure 9.5 summarizes when you might want to consider using each of these types of digests.

2. Locating Topics and Key Numbers

Once you have decided which set or sets of the digest to use, the next step is locating topics and key numbers relevant to your research question. You can do this by using the headnotes in a case on point or the Descriptive-Word Index.

The easiest way to find relevant topics and key numbers is to use the headnotes in a case that you have already determined is relevant to your research. If you have a relevant case that is published in a West reporter, you can use the headnotes to direct you to digest topics and key numbers.

If you do not already have a case on point, you will need to use the index to find topics and key numbers in the digest. The index in a West digest is called the Descriptive-Word Index (DWI). The DWI actually consists of several volumes that may be located either at the beginning or at the end of the digest set, and it lists subjects in alphabetical order.

▼ FIGURE 9.5   When to Use Different Digests

FEDERAL DIGESTS	STATE DIGESTS	REGIONAL DIGESTS	COMBINED DIGESTS
To research federal cases	To research state and federal cases from an individual state	To research state cases from an individual state within a region (may require additional federal digest research)	To research federal cases or cases from an individual state if you know the approximate time period you wish to research
To supplement regional digest research by locating federal cases within an individual state		To locate nonbinding authority from surrounding jurisdictions	To research the law of all jurisdictions within the United States

To use the DWI, all you need to do is look up the subjects you want to research. The subjects will be followed by abbreviations indicating the topics and key numbers relevant to each subject. A list of abbreviations appears at the beginning of the volume.

Once you have identified relevant topics and key numbers, the next step is looking them up within the digest volumes. Digest volumes are organized alphabetically. Therefore, you will need to look on the spines of the books until you locate the volume covering your topic. When you locate the topic in the main digest volume, it may be worthwhile for you to read the topic summary and scan the outline of key numbers to see if other topics and key numbers would be useful for your research.

3. Reading Case Summaries

The next step is reading case summaries under the relevant key number. In general, summaries are organized in descending order from highest to lowest court. If the digest contains summaries of both federal and state cases, federal cases will appear first. If the digest contains summaries of cases from multiple states, the states will be listed alphabetically. Summaries of multiple cases from the same level of court and the same jurisdiction are listed in reverse chronological order.

As with online digest research, one of the most difficult aspects of print digest research is deciding which cases to read based on the summaries. The court and date abbreviations at the beginning of each entry will help you decide which cases to review. If you are using a digest with cases from more than one jurisdiction, paying attention to the abbreviations will help you stay focused on the summaries of cases from the appropriate jurisdiction. The abbreviations will also help you figure out which cases are from the highest court in the jurisdiction and which are the most recent. In addition, many case summaries include not only a synopsis of the rule the court applied in the case, but also a concise description of the facts. You can use the factual summaries to narrow down the cases applicable to your research question. Remember that the digest summaries, like the case headnotes, are not authoritative. Always read a case in full before relying on it to answer a research question.

4. Updating Your Research

The last step is updating your research. Print digest volumes are updated with pocket parts. Some sets also have separate softcover supplements that update the entire digest set. Both the pocket part and any other supplements will be organized by topics and key numbers.

Citators and Other Updating Tools

A. INTRODUCTION ▼

1. The Purpose of a Citator

Virtually all cases contain citations to legal authorities, including other cases, secondary sources, statutes, and regulations. These decisions can affect the continued validity of the authorities they cite. For example, earlier cases can be reversed or overruled, or statutes can be held unconstitutional. Even if an authority remains valid, the discussion of the authority in later cases can be helpful in your research. As a consequence, when you find an authority that helps you answer a research question, you will often want to know whether the authority has been cited elsewhere, and if so, what has been said about it.

The tool that helps you do this is called a citator. Citators catalog cases, secondary sources, and other authorities, analyzing what they say about the sources they cite. Some citators also track the status of statutes and regulations, indicating, for example, whether a statute has been amended or repealed. Citators will help you determine whether an authority is still good law, meaning it has not been changed or invalidated since it was issued. They will also help you locate additional authorities that pertain to your research question.

Shepard's Citations is the best known citator. Shepard's was, for many years, the only citator most lawyers ever used, and checking citations came to be known as "Shepardizing." Generations of law students learned how to interpret Shepard's print entries, which are filled with symbols and abbreviations. Today, however, few legal researchers use Shepard's in print, and few libraries carry the print version. Instead, virtually all legal researchers use online citators. Shepard's is still a well-respected citator, and it is available in Lexis. Westlaw also has its own citator — called KeyCite — and Bloomberg Law has a citator called BCite. Other online service providers may have their own citators.

Citators can be used in researching many types of authority, including cases, statutes, regulations, and some secondary sources. The process of using a citator, however, is the same for almost any type of authority. Accordingly, for purposes of introducing you to this process, this chapter focuses on the use of citators in case research. Later chapters in this book discuss the use of Shepard's and KeyCite in researching other types of authority.

2. When to Use a Citator in Case Research

You must check every case you rely on to make sure it is still good law. In general, you will want to use a citator early in your research, after you have identified what appear to be a few key cases, to make sure you do not build your analysis on authority that is no longer valid. Using a citator at this stage will help direct you to other relevant authorities as well. You should also check every case you cite before handing in written work to make sure each one continues to be authoritative. Citing bad authority is every attorney's nightmare, and failing to check your citations can constitute professional malpractice. As a consequence, now is the time to get in the habit of updating your case research carefully.

3. Terms and Procedural Concepts Used in Citator Research

Before you begin learning how to use citators, it is important to understand the terminology and procedural concepts used in the process. A case citator contains entries for decided cases that list the later authorities (cases, secondary sources, and other forms of authority) that have cited the case. This chapter uses the term "original case" to describe the case that is the subject of the citator entry. The terms "citing case" and "citing source" refer to the later authorities that cite the original case. Thus, for example, if you located the case of *McCracken v. Sloan*, 252 S.E.2d 250, 40 N.C. App. 214 (1979), and wanted to use a citator to verify its continued validity, *McCracken* would be referred to as the original case. The later authorities that cite *McCracken* would be referred to as citing cases (for cases) or citing sources (for all other types of authority).

Two procedural concepts you need to understand are direct and indirect case history. Direct history refers to all of the opinions issued in conjunction with a single piece of litigation. One piece of litigation may generate multiple opinions. A case may be appealed to a higher court, resulting in opinions from both an intermediate appellate court and the court of last resort. A higher court may remand a case — that is, send a case back to a lower court — for reconsideration, again resulting in opinions issued by both courts. Or a court might issue separate opinions to resolve individual matters arising in a case. All of these opinions, whether issued before or after the original case, constitute direct history.

Opinions issued before the original case may be called prior history; those issued after the original case may be called subsequent history or subsequent appellate history, as appropriate. Indirect history refers to an opinion generated from a different piece of litigation than the original case. Every unrelated case that cites the original case is part of the indirect history of the original case.

Both direct and indirect case history can be positive, negative, or neutral. Thus, if the original case is affirmed by a higher court, it has positive direct history, but if the original case is reversed, it has negative direct history. A related opinion in the same litigation on a different issue could be neutral; the opinion resolving the second issue could have no effect on the continued validity of the opinion resolving the first issue. Similarly, if the original case is relied upon by a court deciding a later, unrelated case, the original case has positive indirect history, but if the original case is overruled, it has negative indirect history. A citing case could discuss the original case in a way that does not include any positive or negative analysis. In that situation, the indirect history would be considered neutral.

B. USING A CITATOR FOR CASE RESEARCH _____▼

1. Shepard's in Lexis

To use Shepard's in Lexis effectively, you need to know how to access the service and interpret the entries. One way to access the Shepard's function is by typing *shep:*, followed by the citation you want to Shepardize. Another way is by retrieving a case and following the "*Shepardize®* this document" link.

When you view a Shepard's entry, you must interpret the information provided. One of the first things you will notice is a symbol such as a red stop sign or a yellow triangle. These symbols are called Shepard's Signals, and they indicate the type of treatment the original case has received from the citing cases. If you retrieve the full text of a case before Shepardizing it, you will also see a Shepard's Signal at the beginning of the case. A list of Shepard's Signals and Lexis's definition for each signal appear in Figure 10.1.

It is often difficult to reduce the status of a case to a single notation. Determining the continued validity of an original case often requires study of the citing cases. For example, an original case with a negative Shepard's Signal such as a red stop sign may no longer be good law for one of its points, but it may continue to be authoritative on other points. If you were to rely on the red stop sign without further inquiry, you might miss a case that is important for resolving your research question. As a consequence, although Shepard's Signals can be helpful research tools, you should not rely on them in deciding whether the original case

▼ FIGURE 10.1   Shepard's Signals

SIGNAL	MEANS
Red stop sign	*Warning: Negative treatment indicated* Includes the following analyses: • Overruled by • Superceded by • Abrogated by
Orange square surrounding the letter Q	*Questioned: Validity questioned by citing references* Includes the following analysis: • Questioned by
Yellow triangle	*Caution: Possible negative treatment indicated* Includes the following analyses: • Limited by • Criticized by • Distinguished by
Green diamond surrounding a plus sign	*Positive treatment indicated* Includes the following analyses: • Followed by • Affirmed by
Blue circle surrounding the letter A	*Citing references with analysis available* Other cases cited the case and assigned some analysis that is not considered positive or negative. Includes the following analyses: • Explained by • Cited in a Dissenting Opinion at
Blue circle surrounding the letter I	*Citation information available* References have not applied any analysis to the citation. For example, the case was cited by law reviews that do not have history or treatment analysis. Includes the following analysis: • Cited by

is valid. Always research the Shepard's entry and review the citing cases carefully to satisfy yourself about the status of the original case.

The information in a Shepard's entry is divided into four sections:

- Appellate History;
- Citing Decisions;
- Other Citing Sources; and
- Table of Authorities.

The Appellate History section lists the direct history of the case, meaning prior and subsequent opinions arising from the same litigation. The information in this section will help you determine whether the case is still good law. If a later opinion in the direct line of appeal affects the continued validity of the original case (e.g., reversing or affirming the original case), that information will be noted in the history section. Lexis will also give you a visual snapshot of the original case's history with the Map view. This can be useful if a case has an extensive or complex history.

The Citing Decisions section lists citing cases comprising the indirect history of the original case, i.e., later cases that have cited the original case. The information in this section will help you determine whether the case is still good law. It will also help you identify additional cases that are relevant to your research question.

When you Shepardize a federal case, the Citing Decisions section will begin with U.S. Supreme Court citations, followed by federal cases divided according to circuit. Within each circuit, appellate cases will appear first, followed by federal district court cases. After all of the federal cases, state cases will be listed alphabetically by state, again with cases from higher courts first, followed by those from subordinate courts. When you Shepardize a state case, the Citing Decisions section will begin with cases from the same state as the original case. Then you will see federal cases by circuit and cases from other states.

Along with the full name and citation to the citing case, the entry will note the treatment the citing case has given the original case. Often, the citing case will simply have "cited" the original case without significant analysis. If, however, the citing case has given the original case treatment that could affect its continued validity (e.g., following, criticizing, or distinguishing it), Shepard's will note that.

Lexis has two additional features to show the treatment of the original case. It uses colored blocks next to citing cases to indicate the degree of positive or negative treatment given to the original case. Lexis also allows you to view a color-coded grid that provides a snapshot of the way all of the citing cases have treated the original case.

Another feature in the Citing Decisions section is the headnote references. You may recall from Chapter 9, on case research, that headnotes are summary paragraphs added by case editors identifying the key points in the case. If a citing case cites the original case for a point that is summarized in a headnote at the beginning of the original case, the headnote number will appear in the Shepard's entry. You may again recall from Chapter 9 that Lexis adds its own headnotes — LexisNexis Headnotes — to cases. The LexisNexis Headnotes are the ones displayed in the Shepard's entry.

The Other Citing Sources section lists sources other than cases that have cited the original case. It will help you locate additional information on your research question. The authorities included will depend on where the original case has been cited and may include law reviews, court documents, treatises, and statutory annotations.

The Table of Authorities feature shows how the original case treated the cases it cites. This is useful for determining the strength of the authority upon which the original case relied.

Although the full Shepard's entry provides the most complete information about the original case, you may want to view a more limited entry, depending on your research task. Shepard's offers several menu options for filtering the display to focus on the information most relevant to you, including type of analysis, jurisdiction of citing cases and sources, depth of treatment, headnote, date, or terms you specify.

Another way to check citations is with the brief analyzer tool that Lexis is introducing. This tool is described in Chapter 9 on case research. With this tool, you upload a memorandum, brief, or other document, and the tool analyzes the document's text and citation patterns. In addition to providing targeted research recommendations, the tool also provides a comprehensive Shepard's analysis. You can use this tool with a draft document to generate additional research leads or with a completed document to do a final check of all your citations before submitting your work.

2. KeyCite in Westlaw

To use KeyCite in Westlaw effectively, you need to know how to access the service and interpret the entries. One way to access the KeyCite function is by typing *kc* or *keycite* into the search box, followed by the citation you want to KeyCite. Another way is from a case. KeyCite information for a case appears under tabs accompanying the document.

When you view a KeyCite entry, you must interpret the information provided. KeyCite is linked with cases with a notation system similar to Shepard's Signals. A symbol called a status flag will appear at the beginning of both the case and the KeyCite entry to give you some indication

▼ FIGURE 10.2   Westlaw Status Flags

STATUS FLAG	MEANS
Red flag	The case is no longer good law for at least one of the points it contains.
Yellow flag	The case has some negative history but has not been reversed or overruled.
Blue-striped flag	The case has been appealed to the U.S. Courts of Appeals or the U.S. Supreme Court.
Orange circle surrounding an exclamation point	The case has an overruling risk warning. This means that, although the case has not been formally overruled, it may no longer be good for at least one point of law because it relies on an overruled or otherwise invalid prior decision

of the case's treatment in KeyCite. Westlaw's definitions of the status flags appear in Figure 10.2. Like Shepard's Signals, KeyCite status flags are useful research tools, but they cannot substitute for your own assessment of the continued validity of a case. You should always research the KeyCite entry and review the citing sources carefully to satisfy yourself about the status of a case.

The tabs accompanying a case contain the following KeyCite information:

- Filings — This tab lists the court filings in the original case.
- Negative Treatment — This tab lists both direct and indirect negative history of the original case. If the case has an overruling risk warning, information about the warning also appears here.
- History — This tab shows the direct history of the original case in both list and graphical forms.
- Citing References — This tab shows the complete indirect history of the original case, including citing cases and other citing sources.
- Table of Authorities — This tab shows how the original case treated the cases it cites.

Unlike Shepard's, KeyCite organizes citing sources by depth of treatment, rather than by jurisdiction, although you can vary the display order to sort by date. Westlaw uses a system of green bars to indicate depth of treatment: examined (4 bars); discussed (3 bars); cited (2 bars); and mentioned (1 bar).

Figure 10.3 delineates how West defines these terms. If a citing case quotes the original case, quotation marks will appear after the citation to the citing case in the KeyCite entry.

▼ FIGURE 10.3   KeyCite Depth of Treatment Categories

NUMBER OF BARS	MEANING	DEFINED
Four	Examined	Contains an extended discussion of the original case, usually more than a printed page of text.
Three	Discussed	Contains a substantial discussion of the original case, usually more than a paragraph but less than a printed page.
Two	Cited	Contains some discussion of the original case, usually less than a paragraph.
One	Mentioned	Contains a brief reference to the original case, usually in a string citation.

Headnote references also accompany the citations to citing cases and sources. The headnote references in KeyCite work the same way as those in Shepard's. If a citing source cites the original case for a proposition of law summarized in a headnote at the beginning of the original case, the headnote number will appear in the KeyCite entry. The headnote references in KeyCite correspond only to West headnotes, not to LexisNexis Headnotes.

Although the full KeyCite entry provides the most complete information about the original case, you may want to view a more limited entry depending on your research task. KeyCite offers several menu options for limiting the display to focus on the information most relevant to you, including document type, headnote, terms you specify, jurisdiction, date, or depth of treatment.

Another way to check citations is with Quick Check, a tool described in Chapter 9 on case research. With Quick Check, you upload a memorandum, brief, or other document, and Quick Check evaluates the citations within the document. It produces a report listing KeyCite data for each case in the document, as well as additional cases, secondary sources, and other resources that may be relevant to your research issue. You can use this tool with a draft document to generate additional research leads or with a completed document to do a final check of all your citations before submitting your work.

3. BCite in Bloomberg Law

To use BCite in Bloomberg Law effectively, you need to know how to access the service and interpret the entries. You must first retrieve the text of a case to access BCite information. Then click on BCite Analysis to access the BCite entry.

When you view a BCite entry, you must interpret the information provided. Bloomberg Law uses a system of indicators similar to Shepard's Signals and KeyCite status flags to give you some indication of the case's treatment in BCite. Bloomberg Law's definitions of the indicators appear in Figure 10.4. Like the other citators' symbols, BCite indicators are useful research tools that cannot substitute for your own assessment of the continued validity of a case.

▼ FIGURE 10.4   BCite Indicators

INDICATOR	MEANS
Red box with a white horizontal line	• The case has been reversed, vacated, or depublished. • The court overrules the opinion in full or in part or states that the opinion has been overruled in full or in part by a prior decision.
Orange box with a white circle	• The court states that the opinion has been superseded, displaced, or rendered obsolete by an intervening statute, rule, or regulation.
Yellow box with a white triangle	• The opinion has been modified, clarified, or amended by a subsequent decision. • One or more courts have criticized the legal reasoning of the opinion without overruling it.
Blue box with a white forward slash	• One or more courts have distinguished the opinion on the law or the facts.
Gray box with a white plus sign	• No courts have cited the opinion.
Green box with a white plus sign	• One or more courts cite to, discuss, or follow the opinion with approval.

The BCite entry is divided into four categories:

- Direct History — This tab lists the direct history of the original case.
- Case Analysis — This tab lists citing cases, that is, later cases that have cited the original case.
- Table of Authorities — This tab shows how the original case treated the cases it cites.
- Citing Documents — This tab lists citing sources, that is, all of the legal content within Bloomberg Law that cites the original case.

Unlike Shepard's and KeyCite, BCite organizes citing sources by date, rather than by jurisdiction or depth of treatment. Under Case Analysis, you can change the display order to list cases by citation frequency, the type of citing case analysis (distinguished, discussed, etc.), or court. You can also use menu options to filter the display by a number of criteria, which may include type of case analysis, citation frequency, court, judge, and date. Use the Show Details button to see the references to the original case within the citing cases.

Under the Citing Documents tab, you cannot change the display order, but you can filter by content type or date. Additionally, you can execute a keyword search within the listed documents.

C. CHOOSING AMONG CITATORS ▼

Shepard's and KeyCite are the most widely used citators. BCite is gaining acceptance, but it is not yet as well established as Shepard's and KeyCite. Other online service providers may also offer their own citators. Additionally, Google Scholar includes a How Cited tab with its search results. This is not a citator in the traditional sense, but it is a tool that can refer you to later cases that have cited the original case. Further, although Shepard's and KeyCite provide largely the same information, they are not identical. As a result, you must decide which citator(s) to use for your research.

The decision will depend on several factors. Shepard's and KeyCite are the most accepted citators in legal research, and you should use them whenever you have access to them. Certainly, while you are in law school, you should use both services enough to become comfortable with them. When you are out of school, you may continue to have access to one or both services. Shepard's and KeyCite are fairly economical to use, costing only a few dollars per citation, and some law libraries that have discontinued subscriptions to Shepard's in print provide free public access to these services. If you do not have access to Shepard's or KeyCite but do have access to BCite or another citator, you should use it, understanding that the coverage of the citator may be limited to holdings within that service's database.

Using either Shepard's or KeyCite should be sufficient to verify the continued validity of a case as long as you carefully interpret the information provided. Characterizing the treatment of a case requires the exercise of editorial judgment. From time to time, Shepard's and KeyCite will characterize the status of a case differently. And while both Shepard's and KeyCite are generally reliable, on rare occasions they contain errors. Therefore, if a case is especially important to your analysis, you would do well to check it in more than one citator.

If you are looking for research references, you may also want to use more than one citator. Any citator should provide references to later cases that you can use for research, but not all include references to secondary sources. Shepard's, KeyCite, and BCite include references to secondary sources, but they do not index all the same secondary sources. Thus, you may get different research results in each service. Of course, there is more than one way to find almost any source, so a single citator — even one that does not include references to secondary sources — may be sufficient for your research when used in combination with other research tools. If you are having trouble finding relevant information, however, consider using a different citator to see if it identifies additional research references.

D. STAYING UP TO DATE WITH ALERT SERVICES   ———▼

Sometimes your work on a research project will be done in a few days, but other times it will extend over a longer period of time. In law school, you might work on a moot court brief or scholarly paper for several weeks or even an entire semester. In legal practice, work on individual cases often extends over months or years. When you are working on an issue over a period of time, one online resource that may be useful to you is an alert service. These services automatically run searches and notify you when relevant new information is added to a database. They allow you to stay up to date on developments affecting your research while you are working on a project.

Westlaw offers several alert services. The two that are most likely to be of use to you in law school are KeyCite Alert and WestClip. KeyCite Alert notifies you when new information is added to the KeyCite entries for cases, statutes, federal regulations, or certain federal administrative agency decisions. WestClip allows you to draft a word search to be run periodically in the source(s) you specify and delivers the search results to you. Note, however, that WestClip works only with terms and connectors searches, not descriptive term searches.

Lexis also offers alert services. Shepard's Alert is similar to KeyCite Alert. It notifies you when new information is added to the Shepard's entries for cases, statutes, or federal regulations. A Search Alert runs a word search at specified intervals and delivers the search results to you. The Search Alert function works with terms and connectors or natural language searches.

Bloomberg Law also has a Search Alert function that you can use to run a search on a specified schedule. Other commercial providers frequently offer similar alert services to deliver updates to current events or specified content on a regular basis.

Statutes and Court Rules

A. INTRODUCTION ▼

Statutes enacted by a legislature are organized by subject matter into what is called a "code." Codes are published by jurisdiction; each jurisdiction that enacts statutes collects them in its own code. Thus, the federal government publishes the *United States Code*, which contains all federal statutes, as well as the text of the U.S. Constitution. Statutes for each state are published in individual state codes. Most state codes contain the text of the state constitution, and many include the text of the U.S. Constitution as well.

1. The Publication Process for Federal Statutes

When a federal law is enacted, it is published in three steps: (1) it is published as a separate document; (2) it is included in a chronological listing of all statutes passed within a session of Congress; and (3) it is reorganized by subject matter and placed within the code.

In the first step of the process, every law passed by Congress is assigned a public law number. The public law number indicates the session of Congress in which the law was passed and the order in which it was passed. Thus, Public Law 103-416 was the 416th law passed during the 103rd session of Congress. Each public law is published in a separate booklet or pamphlet containing the full text of the law as it was passed by Congress. This booklet is known as a slip law and is identified by its public law number.

In the second step of the process, slip laws for a session of Congress are compiled together in chronological order. Laws organized within this chronological compilation are called session laws because they are organized according to the session of Congress during which they were enacted. Session laws are compiled in a publication called *United States Statutes at Large*. A citation to *Statutes at Large* will tell you the volume of *Statutes at Large* containing the law and the page number on which the text of the law begins. Thus, a citation to 108 Stat. 4305 tells you that

▼ **FIGURE 11.1** Publication Process for a Federal Statute

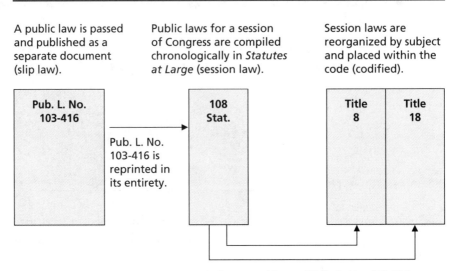

A public law is passed and published as a separate document (slip law).

Public laws for a session of Congress are compiled chronologically in *Statutes at Large* (session law).

Session laws are reorganized by subject and placed within the code (codified).

Pub. L. No. 103-416

Pub. L. No. 103-416 is reprinted in its entirety.

108 Stat.

Title 8

Title 18

Various provisions of Pub. L. No. 103-416 are reprinted within the applicable Titles.

this law can be located in volume 108 of *Statutes at Large*, beginning on page 4305. Both the slip law and session law versions of a statute should be identical. The only difference is the form of publication.

The third step in the process is the codification of the law. When Congress enacts a law, it enacts a block of legislation that may cover a wide range of topics. A single bill can contain provisions applicable to many different parts of the government. For example, a drug abuse prevention law could contain provisions applicable to subject areas such as food and drugs, crimes, and public health. If federal laws remained organized chronologically by the date of passage, it would be virtually impossible to research the law by subject. Laws relating to individual subjects could have been passed at so many different times that it would be extremely difficult to find all of the relevant provisions.

In the third step of the process, therefore, the pieces of the bill are reorganized according to the different subjects they cover, and they are placed by subject, or codified, within the federal code. Once legislation is codified, it is much easier to locate because it can be indexed by subject.

Figure 11.1 illustrates the publication process.

2. The Organization of Statutory Codes

As noted above, a code is a subject matter compilation. A statutory code, therefore, is arranged by subject area. Each subject area is then subdivided into smaller units. A section is the smallest unit of a code.

Although all statutory codes are organized by subject, not all are numbered the same way. The federal code is organized into numbered Titles. Each Title covers a different subject area. Title 18, for instance, contains the laws pertaining to federal crimes, and Title 35 contains the laws pertaining to patents. For many years, the *United States Code* had 50 Titles. In 2010, however, Congress enacted Title 51. As this text goes to press, the federal code has 54 Titles, and additional Titles may be added in the future. Each Title is subdivided into chapters and sections.

To locate a provision of the federal code, you need to know the Title and the section number assigned to it. For example, 18 U.S.C. § 2113 is the provision of the federal code prohibiting bank robbery. The citation tells you that this provision appears in Title 18 of the *United States Code* in section 2113.

A state code can be organized in one of several ways. Some are organized by Title like the federal code. Some have their own unique numbering systems. Some are organized by subject name. Regardless of how the code as a whole is organized, state statutes are typically subdivided into chapters and sections.

To find a provision of a code organized by subject name, you need to know the subject area and the section number assigned to it. For example, New York Penal Law § 190.05 prohibits issuing a bad check. The citation tells you that this provision appears in the Penal Law (the subject area designation for criminal statutes) in section 190.05.

3. Types and Sources of Statutory Codes

Although there is only one code for each jurisdiction, in the sense that each jurisdiction has only one set of statutes in force, the text of the laws may be published by more than one publisher. Sometimes a government arranges for the publication of its laws; this is known as an official code. Sometimes a commercial publisher will publish the laws for a jurisdiction without government authorization; this is known as an unofficial code. Some jurisdictions have both official and unofficial codes, in which case the code will be published in two or more sets of books. Online, the text of a code may be taken from the official code or an unofficial code. If both official and unofficial codes are published for a jurisdiction, they will usually be organized and numbered identically (e.g., all sets will be organized by subject or by Title). For federal laws, the government publishes an official code, *United States Code* or U.S.C. Two unofficial versions of the federal code are also available through commercial publishers, *United States Code Annotated* (U.S.C.A.) and *United States Code Service* (U.S.C.S.).

In addition, a published code can come in one of two formats: annotated or unannotated. An annotated code contains the text of the law, as well as different types of research references. The research references may include summaries of cases or citations to secondary sources discussing a statute. An unannotated code contains only the text of the law. It may have a few references to a statute's history, but other than that, it will not contain research references. As you might imagine, an annotated code is much more useful as a research tool than an unannotated code.

Statutes are available from a number of sources, but not all sources provide access to annotated codes. U.S.C. (the official federal code) is an unannotated code, as are many official state codes. U.S.C. and the official codes for all 50 states and the District of Columbia are publicly available online. You can locate them through government websites or free or commercial legal research services. Unofficial codes are more likely to be annotated. U.S.C.A. and U.S.C.S. are annotated codes. Annotated codes are often available in print at a law library. Westlaw and Lexis provide access to annotated codes, and Bloomberg Law provides access to limited statutory research references.

Federal statutory annotations may include the following categories of information:

- **History:** Contains the history of the section, including summaries of amendments and the public law numbers and *Statutes at Large* citations for the laws containing the revisions. This section can also refer to the legislative history of the statute (for more discussion of legislative history, see Chapter 12).
- **Research references:** Contains references to secondary sources and other materials. It may be divided into sections for digest topics, encyclopedias, law reviews, treatises and other texts, practice aids, and the like (see Chapter 8 for more discussion of secondary sources and Chapter 9 for more discussion of digests).
- **Code of Federal Regulations:** Contains references to administrative agency regulations implementing the statute (for more discussion of administrative regulations, see Chapter 12).
- **Summaries of cases:** Contains summaries of cases interpreting the statute. If the statute has been discussed in a large number of cases, this section may be divided into subject categories.

Figure 11.2 summarizes how different sources organize federal statutory annotations. Annotated state codes contain similar types of information.

Not all sections of an annotated code will contain all of the items listed above, and some will not contain any references at all. The information provided depends on the research references that are appropriate for the specific section of the code.

▼ **FIGURE 11.2**   Information Contained in Federal Statutory Annotations

STATUTORY SOURCE	ANNOTATION CONTENT
Print	Annotations follow the text of the code section: • History & Notes • Library or Research References • Code of Federal Regulations • Notes of Decisions or Notes to Decisions (summaries of cases)
Westlaw	Annotations appear under tabs accompanying the code section: • History tab • Context & Analysis tab (research references; Code of Federal Regulations) • Notes of Decisions tab (summaries of cases)
Lexis	Annotations follow the text of the code section: • History & Notes • Notes to Decisions (summaries of cases) • Research References & Practice Aids (research references; Code of Federal Regulations)
Bloomberg Law	Menu options accompany the code section: • Smart Code (list of cases containing citations to the code section) • Related Content (Code of Federal Regulations for selected federal statutes only)

B. METHODS OF RESEARCHING STATUTES _____▼

You can locate statutes in several ways. If you have the citation to a statute that you have obtained from another source, such as a secondary source, you can easily locate the statute from the citation. When you do not have a citation, you can locate statutes by subject, by words in the document, or by the name of an act.

Print research is good for researching statutes by subject. Consequently, statutes are one form of authority for which lawyers continue to rely, at least in part, on print research. Using an index is one of the most common subject-searching techniques for statutory research. All print codes have subject indexes. Once you locate relevant references to statutory provisions in the index, you can look them up in the main volumes of the code and then update your research with the pocket parts. If you are searching online, you may or may not have access to the index.

Every code also has a table of contents, which you can view in print or online. Reviewing the table of contents can be a difficult way to begin your research unless you know the subject area of the statute you are trying to find. Once you find a relevant provision of the code, however, viewing the table of contents can help you find related code sections, as described more fully below.

Word searching is another way to locate statutes if you search online. Because legislatures often use technical terms in statutes, however, word searching can be more difficult than subject searching if you are not already familiar with the statutory terminology. If you execute a word search in a database that includes an annotated version of a code, the search engine will retrieve documents that contain your search terms not only in the text of the statute but also in any of the annotations. Sometimes this is an advantage in your research. If the statute uses technical terms that are not in your search but the research references describe the concepts using the terms from your search, executing a search that includes the annotations can improve your search results. But sometimes searching for terms within both statutes and annotations can retrieve irrelevant results.

An additional search option is locating a statute by name. Many statutes are known by their popular names, such as the Americans with Disabilities Act. Online, you can use a statute's name as a word search; many services also have directories of statutes listed by popular name. Print codes also have popular name tables or lists you can use to locate a statute by name.

If you execute an unfiltered search in Westlaw, Lexis, or Bloomberg Law, your search results will include statutes. You will ordinarily pre-filter your search by jurisdiction unless you are researching the law of all U.S. jurisdictions. Once you execute the search, the results will include a section with statutes. When you view the statutes your search retrieved, you can filter the results according to a number of criteria.

Most search techniques will lead you to individual sections of a code. But a piece of legislation ordinarily will not appear in its entirety within a single code section. More often, a statutory scheme enacted by a legislature will be codified in a chapter or subchapter of the code comprising multiple code sections. Rarely will an individual code section viewed in isolation resolve your research question. You usually need to research the entire statutory scheme to ensure that you consider all potentially applicable code sections.

Because online searches retrieve individual code sections as separate documents, it is especially easy to lose sight of the need to research multiple sections. For example, assume you retrieved a code provision applicable to your research question but failed to retrieve a nearby section containing definitions of terms used in the applicable provision. If you relied only on the one section your initial search revealed, your research would not be accurate.

Once you have located a relevant code section, the easiest way to research a statutory scheme is to use the statutory outline or table of contents to identify related code provisions. Online services usually display or provide links to statutory outlines or tables of contents, as well as functions that allow you to browse preceding and subsequent code sections. In print, you will often find an outline of sections at the beginning of a chapter or subchapter. And of course, all you have to do is turn the pages to see preceding and subsequent code sections.

Regardless of your search method, be sure to check the date of any statutory material you use. Statutory compilations available online may not be kept up to date or may be updated only as frequently as official print sources. Commercial services include information about how current their statutory materials are. If the material is not up to date, you will need to update your research, as explained in the next section.

C. USING A CITATOR FOR STATUTORY RESEARCH _____▼

Chapter 10 discusses citators and how to use them in conducting case research. Citators are also available as research and updating tools for state and federal statutes. Statutory citator entries typically include information about the history of a statute (i.e., whether it has been amended or repealed), as well as lists of citing cases and sources. Shepard's for statutes is available in Lexis; KeyCite for statutes is available in Westlaw. As this text goes to press, Bloomberg Law's BCite is available only for cases.

Using a citator in statutory research is useful in two situations. First, citators can provide you with the most complete research references for statutory research. As noted above, some sources provide access only to unannotated versions of codes. If you do not have access to an annotated code, a citator is a useful tool for locating cases interpreting a statute. Even if you are using an annotated code, the statutory annotations rarely list every case or other source that has cited the statute. If the annotations are too sparse to give you the information you need about a statute, you may find more complete information in a citator.

Second, citators are updated more frequently than other sources. Therefore, a citator may provide you with the most recent information about the history of the statute (such as any amendments), as well as the most recent research references. Just as you would not want to cite a case that is no longer good law, you would not want to cite a statute that has been repealed or declared unconstitutional. Using a citator, therefore, is the better practice in statutory research.

The process of using KeyCite and Shepard's for statutes is virtually identical to the process of using those services for cases. In Westlaw, KeyCite information is automatically included under the History and

Citing References tabs when you view a code section. The History section lists amendments and other legislative action affecting the statute, along with legislative history documents if they are available. The Citing References section lists every case or other source that has cited the statute. You can limit the display to focus on the information most relevant to your research, and you can monitor a statutory KeyCite entry by creating a KeyCite Alert.

In Lexis, you can access the Shepard's function from a statute you are viewing. A Shepard's statutory entry is divided into three sections: History, Citing Decisions, and Other Citing Sources. The History section shows the history of the statute, indicating, for example, whether the statute has been amended. The Citing Decisions section lists cases that have cited the statute, and the Other Citing Sources section lists law review articles, treatises, and other forms of authority that have cited the statute. You can limit the display to focus on the information most relevant to your research, and you can monitor a statutory Shepard's entry with Shepard's Alert.

D. RESEARCHING RULES OF PROCEDURE ⎯⎯⎯⎯⎯⎯▼

You are probably learning about rules of procedure governing cases filed in court in your Civil Procedure class. Whenever you are preparing to file a document or take some action that a court requires or permits, the court's rules of procedure will tell you how to accomplish your task. The rules of procedure for most courts are published as part of the code for the jurisdiction where the court is located. For example, the Federal Rules of Civil Procedure appear as an appendix to Title 28 in the federal code. In many states, court procedural rules are published in a separate Rules volume.

If you want to locate procedural rules, therefore, one way to find them is through the applicable code. Many procedural rules have been interpreted by the courts, so you might need to research cases to understand the rules' requirements fully. If you locate rules in an annotated code, summaries of the decisions will follow the rules, just as they do any other provision of the code.

Three caveats about locating rules of procedure are in order. First, understanding the rules can be challenging. As with any other type of research, you may want to research secondary sources for commentary on the rules and citations to cases interpreting the rules to make sure you understand them. For the Federal Rules of Civil Procedure, two helpful treatises are *Moore's Federal Practice* and Wright & Miller's *Federal Practice and Procedure*. For state procedural rules, a state "deskbook," or handbook containing practical information for lawyers practicing in the jurisdiction, may contain both the text of the rules and helpful commentary. If you locate the rules through a secondary source, however, be sure to update your research because the rules can be amended at any time.

Second, virtually all jurisdictions have multiple types and levels of courts, and each of these courts may have its own procedural rules. Therefore, be sure you locate the rules for the appropriate court. Determining which court is the appropriate one may require separate research into the jurisdiction of the courts.

Third, many individual districts, circuits, or divisions of courts have local rules that you must follow. Local rules cannot conflict with the rules of procedure published with the code, but they may add requirements that do not appear in the rules of procedure. Local rules usually are not published with the code, but you can obtain them from a number of sources, including the court's website, a secondary source such as a practice deskbook, or an online service. To be sure that your work complies with the court's rules, do not neglect any local rules that may add to the requirements spelled out in the rules of procedure.

Federal Legislative History and Administrative Regulations

Two forms of authority you should become familiar with are federal legislative history documents and federal administrative regulations. When Congress passes a statute, the paper trail of documents leading to its passage is called legislative history. The information in a statute's legislative history can be useful in interpreting an ambiguous statute. Additionally, as explained in Chapter 2, when Congress legislates, it often delegates to administrative agencies the responsibility of enforcing the statute. To do this, agencies adopt administrative regulations that implement the statute's requirements. This chapter discusses how to research federal legislative history documents and administrative regulations.

A. FEDERAL LEGISLATIVE HISTORY ▼

1. Introduction

When a legislature passes a statute, it does so with a goal in mind, such as prohibiting or regulating certain types of conduct. Despite their best efforts, however, legislators do not always draft statutes that express their intentions clearly, and it is almost impossible to draft a statute that contemplates every possible situation that may arise under it. Accordingly, lawyers and judges are often called upon to determine the meaning of an ambiguous statute. Lawyers must provide guidance about what the statute permits or requires their clients to do. In deciding cases, judges must determine what the legislature intended when it passed the statute.

If you are asked to analyze an ambiguous statute, you have a number of tools available to help with the task. If the courts have already resolved the ambiguity, secondary sources, statutory annotations, citators, or other research resources can lead you to cases that explain the meaning of the statute.

If the ambiguity has not yet been resolved, however, you face a bigger challenge. You could research similar statutes to see if they shed light on the provision you are interpreting. You could also look to the language of the statute itself for guidance. You may have studied analytical tools called "canons of construction" in some of your other classes. These canons are principles used to determine the meaning of a statute. For example, one canon provides that statutory terms are to be construed according to their ordinary and plain meaning. Another states that remedial statutes are to be broadly construed, while criminal statutes are to be narrowly construed. Although these tools can be helpful in interpreting statutes, they rarely provide the complete answer to determining the legislature's intent.

One of the best ways to determine legislative intent is to research the paper trail of documents that legislators create during the legislative process. These documents are known as the legislative history of the statute. This chapter discusses various types of documents that make up a statute's legislative history and explains how to locate and use them. At the state level, the types of legislative history documents produced and their ease of accessibility vary widely; therefore, this chapter discusses only federal legislative history.

2. The Process of Enacting a Federal Law

"Legislative history" is a generic term used to refer to a variety of documents produced during the legislative process; it does not refer to a single document or research tool. Courts consider some legislative history documents more important than others, depending on the type of information in the document and the point in the legislative process when the document was created. Understanding what legislative history consists of, as well as the value of different legislative history documents, requires an understanding of the legislative process.

The legislative process begins when a bill is introduced into the House of Representatives or the Senate by a member of Congress. After the bill is introduced, it is usually referred to a committee. The committee can hold hearings on the bill to obtain the views of experts and interested parties, or it can refer the bill to a subcommittee to hold hearings. If the committee is not in favor of the bill, it usually takes no action. This ordinarily causes the bill to expire in the committee, although the sponsor is free to reintroduce the bill in a later session of Congress. If the committee is in favor of the bill, it will recommend passage to the full chamber of the House or Senate. The recommendation is presented in a committee report that contains the full text of the bill and an analysis of each provision. Because the committee presents its views in a report, this process is called "reporting" the bill.

The bill then goes before the full House or Senate, where it is debated and may be amended. The members of the House or Senate vote on the bill. If it is passed, the bill goes before the other chamber of Congress, where the same process is repeated. If both chambers pass the bill, it goes to the President. The President can sign the bill into law, allow it to become law without a signature, or veto it. If the bill is vetoed, it goes back to Congress. Congress can override the President's veto if two-thirds of the House and the Senate vote in favor of the bill. Once a bill is passed into law, it is assigned a public law number and proceeds through the publication process described in Chapter 11, on statutory research.

This is a simplified explanation of how legislation is enacted. A bill may make many detours along this path before becoming a law or being defeated. One situation that often occurs is that the House and Senate will pass slightly different versions of the same bill. When this happens, the bill is sent to what is called a conference committee. The conference committee consists of members of both houses of Congress, and its job is to attempt to reconcile the two versions of the bill. If the committee members are able to agree on the provisions of the bill, the compromise version is sent back to both chambers of Congress to be reapproved. If both houses approve the compromise bill, it then goes to the President.

Documents created at each stage of this process constitute the legislative history of a law. The next section describes the major sources that make up a legislative history.

3. Types of Federal Legislative History Documents

There are four major types of federal legislative history documents:

- the bills introduced in Congress;
- hearings before committees or subcommittees;
- floor debates in the House and the Senate;
- committee reports.

These documents are listed in order from least authoritative to most authoritative. Although some of these sources are generally considered to have more weight than others, none should be viewed in isolation. Each item contributes to the documentation of the legislature's intent. In fact, you may find that the documents contain information that is either contradictory or equally as ambiguous as the underlying statute. It is rare when an inquiry into legislative history will give you a definitive answer to a question of statutory interpretation. What is more likely is that the documents will equip you with information you can use to support your arguments for the proper interpretation of the statute.

a. Bills

The bill as originally introduced into Congress can be compared with any later versions of the bill to try to determine congressional intent.

Changes in language and addition or deletion of specific provisions may shed light on the goal the legislature was attempting to accomplish with the bill. Analysis of changes to a bill, however, requires speculation about the reasons behind the changes. Consequently, this is often considered an insufficient indication of legislative intent unless it is combined with other materials indicating intent to achieve a particular objective.

b. Hearings

Hearings before committees and subcommittees consist of the testimony of experts and interested parties called to give their views on the bill. Documents from these hearings may contain transcripts of testimony, reports, studies, or any other information requested by or submitted to the hearing committee. Unlike interpretation of different versions of a bill, interpretation of hearings does not require speculation. The individuals or groups providing information usually give detailed explanations and justifications for their positions.

Congress uses hearings to gather information. As a consequence, individuals or groups with opposing views are often represented, and their goal is to persuade Congress to act in a particular way. This results in the inclusion of information both for and against the legislation in the hearing documents. Sometimes it is possible to ascertain whether material from a particular source motivated Congress to act in a particular way, but this is not always the case. Therefore, hearing documents must be used carefully in determining congressional intent.

c. Floor Debates

Floor debates are another source of legislative history. They are published in a daily record of congressional proceedings called the *Congressional Record.* Unlike hearings, which include commentary that may or may not have been persuasive to the committee, floor debates consist of statements by the legislators themselves. Thus, the debates can be a source of information about Congress's intent in passing a bill. Debates may consist of transcripts of comments or exchanges taking place on the floor of Congress. In addition, members of Congress are permitted to submit prepared statements setting forth their views. Statements by a bill's sponsors may be especially useful in determining legislative intent. Different members of Congress may give different reasons for supporting legislation, however, and they are permitted to amend or supplement their statements after the fact. As a consequence, floor debates are not a definitive source for determining legislative intent.

d. Committee Reports

Committee reports are generally considered to be the most authoritative legislative history documents. They usually contain the committee's reasons for recommending the bill, a section-by-section analysis of the bill, and the views of any committee members who dissent from the committee's conclusions. If a bill is sent to a conference committee to work out compromise language, the conference committee usually prepares a report. This report discusses only the provisions that differed before the House and the Senate. It usually contains the agreed-upon language of the bill and an explanation of the compromise.

4. Methods of Researching Federal Legislative History Documents

You can locate federal legislative history documents the same ways you locate most other forms of legal authority: by citation; by subject; and, for documents available online, by words in the document. Although federal legislative history documents have their own citations, those created in conjunction with legislation that is enacted into law are often organized by the bill number, public law number, or *Statutes at Large* citation associated with the legislation. Not all federal legislative history documents, however, are associated with legislation enacted into law. As a consequence, the methods you choose to research federal legislative history will depend on the type of material you need. If you are researching the history of an individual statute, your approach will be different than if you are looking for legislative activity on a particular subject.

If you are researching the history of an individual statute, it is important to remember that not all legislation is accompanied by all of the documents described above. A committee might elect not to hold hearings. Or the bill could be amended during floor debate, in which case the amendment would not have any history to be documented elsewhere. In addition, you may not always need to look at all of these documents to resolve your research question. If you are trying to determine Congress's intent in enacting a specific provision within a statute, and a committee report sets out the goals Congress was attempting to accomplish with that provision, you might not need to go any further in your research. Often, however, the committee reports will not discuss the provision you need to interpret. In that case, you may need to delve further into the legislative history, reviewing floor debates or hearings to see if the provision was discussed in either of those sources. In other instances, you may need to compile a complete legislative history.

Your research path will depend largely on the scope of your assignment. You will almost always begin with the statute itself. From there, you should be able to use the bill number, public law number, or *Statutes at Large* citation to locate documents relating to the statute. In most cases, you will probably want to begin by reviewing committee reports. If the committee reports do not address your question, you will then need to assess which other sources of legislative history are likely to assist you and which research tools provide the most efficient means of accessing those documents. If your research takes you beyond readily accessible committee reports, you may want to consult with a reference librarian for assistance in compiling the relevant documents. Remember also that a statute may be amended after its original enactment. Legislative history documents related to any amendments will be associated with the bill numbers, public law numbers, or *Statutes at Large* citations of the amending legislation.

If you are trying to find out about legislative activity on a specific topic, rather than the history of an individual statute, you will need to conduct subject or word searches. Because most bills are not passed into law, you may find documents relating to bills that have expired. In addition, you may locate documents unrelated to a bill. For example, a committee may hold hearings on a matter within its jurisdiction, even if no legislation on the matter has been introduced.

Some research tools lend themselves more easily than others to subject and word searching, and some are more comprehensive in their coverage than others. Therefore, you will need to determine how much information you need, such as whether you need information on bills that have expired as well as existing legislation, and how far back in time you want to search. You would be well advised to consult with a reference librarian for assistance in developing your research plan for this type of research.

a. Compiled Legislative Histories in Print

Legislative histories for major pieces of legislation are sometimes compiled and published as separate volumes. In this situation, an author or publisher collects all of the legislative history documents on the legislation and publishes them in a single place. If the legislative history on the statute you are researching has already been compiled, your work has been done for you. Therefore, if you are researching a major piece of legislation, you should begin by looking for a compiled legislative history.

There are two ways to locate a compiled legislative history in print. The first is to look in the online catalog in your library. Compiled legislative histories can be published as individual books that are assigned call numbers and placed on the shelves. The second is to look for the statute in a reference source listing compiled legislative histories. Two excellent options are *Sources of Compiled Legislative Histories: A Bibliography of Government Documents, Periodical Articles, and Books, 1st Congress-114th Congress* and *Federal Legislative Histories: An Annotated Bibliography and Index to Officially Published Sources.*

b. Government Sources

The federal government provides free online access to many legislative history documents through Congress.gov and govinfo.gov.

Congress.gov is a website maintained by the Library of Congress. It will provide you with the text of bills introduced, House and Senate roll call votes, public laws, the text of the *Congressional Record*, committee reports, and other information on the legislative process. An effective way to locate the history of an individual piece of legislation is by searching with the public law or bill number. Congress.gov will retrieve an overview page with information about the legislation. Below the overview you will find tabs with links to the text of the statute and to all of the legislative history documents in Congress.gov's database, including congressional reports and floor debates in the *Congressional Record*. This site does not include congressional hearings or testimony, but the Resources directory has links to sources with these materials.

Govinfo.gov is a website maintained by the Government Printing Office (GPO). It is the official repository of digital government content, and it contains legislative history information. Govinfo.gov provides access to the text of bills introduced into Congress, selected reports and hearings, and the *Congressional Record*. You can find a document by searching or browsing. If your research results include public laws, the Details link following the document summary will list legislative history documents.

Govinfo.gov is a good source to use to access congressional hearings. The hearing documents are.pdf versions of the print documents. Thus, unlike some other online sources, govinfo.gov provides the complete hearing content, including attachments and other documents, not just testimony.

c. Commercial Services

HeinOnline and ProQuest Congressional are two commercial subscription services available through a subscribing library's research portal that you can use for federal legislative history research. HeinOnline is best known for its comprehensive database of legal periodicals, but it also contains many other types of information, including legislative documents. HeinOnline has a database of compiled legislative histories derived from the well-known reference book, *Sources of Compiled Legislative Histories: A Bibliography of Government Documents, Periodical Articles, and Books*. This database provides citations to many compiled legislative histories and full-text access to some. HeinOnline also has its own collection of compiled legislative histories, the U.S. Federal Legislative History Title Collection. This is a database containing full-text legislative histories on major pieces of legislation. Many of these compiled legislative histories contain complete.pdf versions of the legislative documents, including hearings.

ProQuest Congressional is a commercial research service that provides online access to a comprehensive set of legislative documents. Its database includes compiled legislative histories, committee reports, hearing testimony, complete hearings, bills, and the *Congressional Record*. The specific content a user can access varies according to the type of subscription. Within ProQuest Congressional, the easiest way to locate all of the available documents on a piece of legislation is to search by number using the bill number, public law number, or *Statutes at Large* citation. Searching this way retrieves an entry that lists the legislative history documents associated with the statute. The links in the list will retrieve the full text of documents.

Westlaw, Lexis, and Bloomberg Law provide access to some federal legislative history documents. In Westlaw and Lexis, the annotations accompanying federal statutes may refer to legislative history information.

B. FEDERAL ADMINISTRATIVE REGULATIONS _____▼

1. Introduction

Administrative agencies exist at all levels of government. Examples of federal administrative agencies include the Food and Drug Administration (FDA), the Environmental Protection Agency (EPA), and the Federal Communications Commission (FCC). Agencies are created by statute, but they are part of the executive branch because they enforce or implement a legislatively created scheme. In creating an agency, a legislature will pass what is known as "enabling" legislation. Enabling legislation defines the scope of the agency's mission and enables it to perform its functions, which may include adopting regulations and adjudicating controversies, among other functions. If an agency is empowered to adopt regulations, those regulations cannot exceed the authority granted by the legislature. Thus, for example, while the FCC may be able to establish regulations concerning television licenses, it would not be able to adopt regulations concerning the labeling of drugs because that would exceed the authority granted to it by Congress in its enabling legislation.

Federal agencies often adopt regulations to implement statutes passed by Congress. Sometimes Congress cannot legislate with the level of detail necessary to implement a complex legislative scheme. In those circumstances, Congress charges an agency with enforcing the statute, and the agency will develop procedures for implementing more general legislative mandates. In the Family and Medical Leave Act, for instance, Congress mandated that an employer allow an employee with a "serious health condition" to take unpaid medical leave. Pursuant to the statute, the Department of Labor has adopted more specific regulations defining what "serious health condition" means.

In format, a regulation looks like a statute. It is, in essence, a rule created by a government entity, and many times administrative regulations are called "rules." In operation, they are indistinguishable from statutes, although the methods used to create, modify, and repeal them are different from those applicable to statutes.

2. The Process of Adopting a Federal Regulation

Federal administrative agencies are required to conform to the procedures set out in the Administrative Procedure Act (APA) in adopting regulations. (State agencies may be required to comply with similar statutes at the state level.) Without going into too much detail, the APA frequently requires agencies to undertake the following steps: (1) notify the public when they plan to adopt new regulations or change existing ones; (2) publish proposed regulations and solicit comments on them before the regulations become final; and (3) publish final regulations before they go into effect to notify the public of the new requirements.

At the federal level, regulations and proposed regulations are published in the *Federal Register.* The *Federal Register* is a daily publication reporting the activities of the executive branch of government. A new volume is published each year. It begins on the first business day of the new year with page one and is consecutively paginated from that point on until the last business day of the year.

After final regulations are published in the *Federal Register*, they are codified in the *Code of Federal Regulations* (C.F.R.). The C.F.R. is divided into 50 Titles. The C.F.R. Titles are subdivided into chapters, which are usually named for the agencies issuing the regulations. Chapters are subdivided into Parts covering specific regulatory areas, and Parts are further subdivided into sections. To find a regulation, you would need to know its Title and section number. A citation to 7 C.F.R. § 210.1 tells you that the regulation is published in Title 7 of the C.F.R. in Part 210, section number 210.1.

The C.F.R. is updated once a year in four separate installments. Titles 1 through 16 are updated on January 1 of each year, Titles 17 through 27 on April 1, Titles 28 through 41 on July 1, and Titles 42 through 50 on October 1. Because a new set of C.F.R. volumes is published annually, the print C.F.R. is not updated with pocket parts. Instead, new or amended regulations are published in the *Federal Register*. They are then codified within the C.F.R. when a new set is published.

3. Methods of Researching Federal Regulations

You can locate federal regulations in several ways. Three common techniques are searching by citation, by subject, or by words in the document.

One way to find citations to relevant regulations is through annotations in U.S.C.A. or U.S.C.S. Because regulations implement statutory schemes, you will often begin regulatory research by consulting the relevant statute, and the statute's annotations may include citations to regulations. The annotations will not ordinarily direct you to a specific regulation; instead, they will direct you to the Title and Part of the C.F.R. with regulations applicable to the area of law you are researching.

Researching by subject is another useful way to locate regulations. You can search by subject in print using the index to the C.F.R. The index entries will refer you to Titles and Parts or sections of the C.F.R. relevant to different subject areas. If you are searching online, you may or may not have access to the index.

Each Title and Part of the C.F.R. has a table of contents, which you can use to browse by subject. Reviewing the table of contents can be a difficult way to begin your research unless you know which agency adopted the regulations you are trying to find. Once you find a relevant regulation, however, viewing the table of contents can help you find related regulations, as described more fully below.

Word searching is another way to locate regulations when you search online. You can execute a word search in a database limited to federal regulations. If you do an unfiltered search in Westlaw, Lexis, or Bloomberg Law that includes federal materials, federal regulations will appear in the search results. Because regulators often use technical terms in regulations, however, word searching can be more difficult than subject searching if you are not already familiar with the regulatory terminology.

Two additional avenues for regulatory research are the telephone and e-mail. Agency staff can be an invaluable resource for understanding the agency's operations, as well as for staying up to date on the agency's activities. If you practice in an area of law subject to agency regulation, do not hesitate to contact agency staff for information. Regulatory notices published in the *Federal Register* typically provide the name and contact information of an agency staff member who can provide additional information about the regulations.

Regulatory research is similar to statutory research in two ways. First, you will often need to research interrelated regulations, not individual sections of the C.F.R., to answer your research question. Therefore, regardless of the search method you use initially to locate a relevant regulation, you should plan to expand your search to consider the entire regulatory scheme. Because online searches retrieve individual regulations as separate documents, it is important to be mindful of the need to research multiple sections. You can view the detailed outline of sections at the beginning of the Part to see the full regulatory scheme. Second, many federal regulations have been interpreted by the courts, so you will often need to research cases to understand the regulations' requirements fully.

4. Sources of Federal Regulations

a. Government Sources

Because the C.F.R. and *Federal Register* are government publications, they are available online. Govinfo.gov is one of the best places to research federal regulations, especially because it provides the official version of the C.F.R. in .pdf format. You can enter a citation, execute a word search from the govinfo.gov home page, or go to the *Code of Federal Regulations* page to browse by Title. Sites for individual agencies can also be good sources for federal regulations.

If you use a government source to locate C.F.R. provisions, pay careful attention to the date of the material you are using. Government sources of regulations are usually updated on the same schedule as the print version of the C.F.R. At govinfo.gov, for example, the official C.F.R. database is updated four times per year as the new print editions of the C.F.R. become available, although the *Federal Register* database is updated daily.

The GPO offers an unofficial version of the C.F.R. called the *Electronic Code of Federal Regulations* (e-CFR). The e-CFR is updated daily to incorporate changes to regulations as they are published in the *Federal Register*. Although the e-CFR is not an official source for regulations, it is a useful research tool. By comparing the official C.F.R. text with the e-CFR version, you can determine quickly and easily whether a regulation has been changed since the latest official edition of the C.F.R. was published. If the regulation has been changed, the e-CFR will provide the citation to the *Federal Register* page containing the change following the text of the regulation. If you need an official source and citation for the change, you can then use govinfo.gov to retrieve the relevant *Federal Register* page. You can access the e-CFR in three ways: (1) going directly to the e-CFR site; (2) following the link on the govinfo.gov *Code of Federal Regulations* page; or (3) browsing the govinfo.gov collection and following the link in the directory.

Although no reason exists to doubt the accuracy of the e-CFR, there may be times when, out of an abundance of caution, you want to double check your research by updating it with official government sources. Govinfo.gov also provides access to a monthly publication called the *List of CFR Sections Affected* (LSA). The LSA is a directory of C.F.R. sections affected by agency action. It provides the citations to the pages in the *Federal Register* that contain changes to federal regulations.

b. Commercial Services

Commercial services, including Westlaw, Lexis, and Bloomberg Law, provide access to the C.F.R. Both Westlaw and Lexis offer annotated versions of the C.F.R. The C.F.R. annotations contain references to secondary sources, cases, and other information and are similar to statutory annotations. In Bloomberg Law, the SmartCode tab accompanying a regulation provides references to cases that have cited the provision. Other commercial services provide access only to the regulations in the C.F.R.

If you research with a commercial service, it is important to be aware of how the service updates the C.F.R. If the service provides access to the official version of the C.F.R., updating your research requires you to research the *Federal Register* for any regulatory changes.

Like the e-CFR, Westlaw, Lexis, and Bloomberg Law incorporate changes to regulations as they appear in the *Federal Register* so that the version of the C.F.R. you see in these services is ordinarily up to date. You can verify the date through which the regulation is updated by checking the updating date at the beginning or end of the document. The *Federal Register* is also available in these services, although the continuous updating of the C.F.R. usually makes it unnecessary to use the *Federal Register* for updating regulations. The continuous updates also mean, however, that the version of the C.F.R. in these services is not the official version. If you need an official version of a regulation, you must use a different source, such as govinfo.gov.

5. Using a Citator for Regulatory Research

Chapter 10 discusses citators and how to use them in conducting case research. Shepard's and KeyCite are also available for researching federal regulations. Regulatory citator entries will list *Federal Register* entries affecting the regulation and list cases and other sources that have cited a regulation.

Using a citator in regulatory research is especially useful for locating research references. As noted above, not all sources provide access to an annotated version of the C.F.R.; many provide access only to unannotated regulations. Therefore, a citator is a useful tool for locating cases or other authorities interpreting a regulation. Even if you are using an annotated version of the C.F.R., the regulatory annotations often do not list every case or other source that has cited the regulation. If the annotations are too sparse to give you the information you need about a regulation, you may find more complete information in a citator.

Research Flowcharts

The research flowcharts that follow are intended to help you develop a coherent research strategy. You can use them in conjunction with your pre-search filtering to plan your research path and with your post-search filtering to focus on the most relevant authorities.

A. GENERAL RESEARCH FLOWCHART

Flowchart A is a general flowchart adaptable to any type of research project.

As Chapter 4 explains, the goal of your pre-search filtering should be to use the information you already have to narrow the field of all legal information before you begin looking for authority. As you can see from Flowchart A, the more you can narrow the field of legal information at the start, the further down the process you can begin. If you know nothing about the subject, you will probably need to begin with secondary sources, either by choosing a particular secondary source or by reviewing the secondary sources retrieved from an unfiltered search. If you already have a citation to an authority on point, you can use that as a starting point.

Once you have a sense of the legal doctrine applicable to your research question, you may also have a sense of whether the issue is a common-law issue governed by case law or an issue to which statutes, regulations, or other types of authority might apply. You can use this information to determine the best starting point for researching individual types of primary authority and the appropriate criteria for post-search filtering.

▼ **FLOWCHART A**   General Research Flowchart

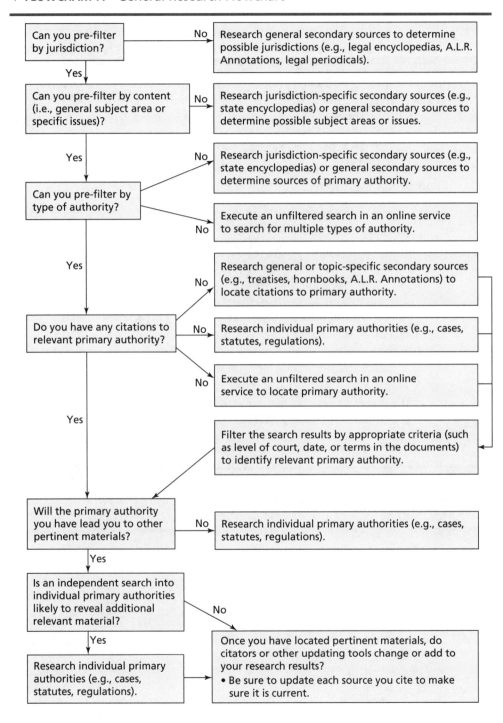

B. NONBINDING AUTHORITY RESEARCH FLOWCHART

You will not always know at the beginning of a research project whether you need to search for nonbinding authority. As you conduct your research, however, you might determine that you need to search for nonbinding authority to analyze your research question thoroughly. Flowchart B is a guide to researching nonbinding authority.

The first thing you need to determine in your pre-search filtering process for nonbinding authority is why you are searching for nonbinding authority. Nonbinding authority can serve a variety of purposes in your analysis of a research question. Here are four common reasons why you would want to research nonbinding authority:

- When you want to buttress an analysis largely resolved by binding primary authorities.
- When the applicable legal rules are clearly defined by binding primary authorities, but the specific factual situation has not arisen in the controlling jurisdiction. You might want to try to locate factually analogous cases from other jurisdictions.
- When the applicable rule is unclear and you want to make an analogy to another area of law to support your analysis.
- When the question is one of first impression in the controlling jurisdiction for which no governing rule exists. In this case, you might want to find out how other jurisdictions have addressed the issue, or if no jurisdiction has faced the question, whether any commentators have analyzed the issue.

Once you know why you need nonbinding authority, one strategy to consider is taking a second look at any nonbinding authorities you located in your initial search efforts. If the authorities you have already located prove sufficient, you should update your research to make sure everything you cite remains authoritative and, if appropriate, end your search for nonbinding authority.

On the other hand, you might review the results of your research and determine that you need to undertake a separate search for nonbinding authority. Flowchart B illustrates several research avenues for locating nonbinding authority.

▶ **FLOWCHART B   Searching for Nonbinding Authority**

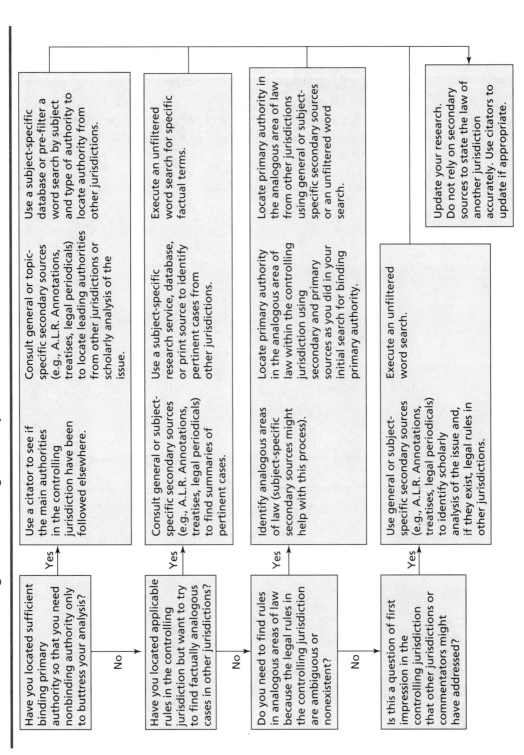

Have you located sufficient binding primary authority so that you need nonbinding authority only to buttress your analysis?

No → **Yes** →

Use a citator to see if the main authorities in the controlling jurisdiction have been followed elsewhere.

Consult general or topic-specific secondary sources (e.g., A.L.R. Annotations, treatises, legal periodicals) to locate leading authorities from other jurisdictions or scholarly analysis of the issue.

Use a subject-specific database or pre-filter a word search by subject and type of authority to locate authority from other jurisdictions.

Have you located applicable rules in the controlling jurisdiction but want to try to find factually analogous cases in other jurisdictions?

No → **Yes** →

Consult general or subject-specific secondary sources (e.g., A.L.R. Annotations, treatises, legal periodicals) to find summaries of pertinent cases.

Use a subject-specific research service, database, or print source to identify pertinent cases from other jurisdictions.

Execute an unfiltered word search for specific factual terms.

Do you need to find rules in analogous areas of law because the legal rules in the controlling jurisdiction are ambiguous or nonexistent?

No → **Yes** →

Identify analogous areas of law (subject-specific secondary sources might help with this process).

Locate primary authority in the analogous area of law within the controlling jurisdiction using secondary and primary sources as you did in your initial search for binding primary authority.

Locate primary authority in the analogous area of law from other jurisdictions using general or subject-specific secondary sources or an unfiltered word search.

Is this a question of first impression in the controlling jurisdiction that other jurisdictions or commentators might have addressed?

No → **Yes** →

Use general or subject-specific secondary sources (e.g., A.L.R. Annotations, treatises, legal periodicals) to identify scholarly analysis of the issue and, if they exist, legal rules in other jurisdictions.

Execute an unfiltered word search.

Update your research. Do not rely on secondary sources to state the law of another jurisdiction accurately. Use citators to update if appropriate.

C.   FLOWCHARTS FOR FOUR COMMON TYPES OF RESEARCH

The flowcharts that follow are tailored to four common types of research: state common-law research, state statutory research, federal statutory research, and federal and state procedural research. When you can pre-filter your research by one of these types of authority, these flowcharts can guide you through the research process.

1. STATE COMMON-LAW RESEARCH FLOWCHART

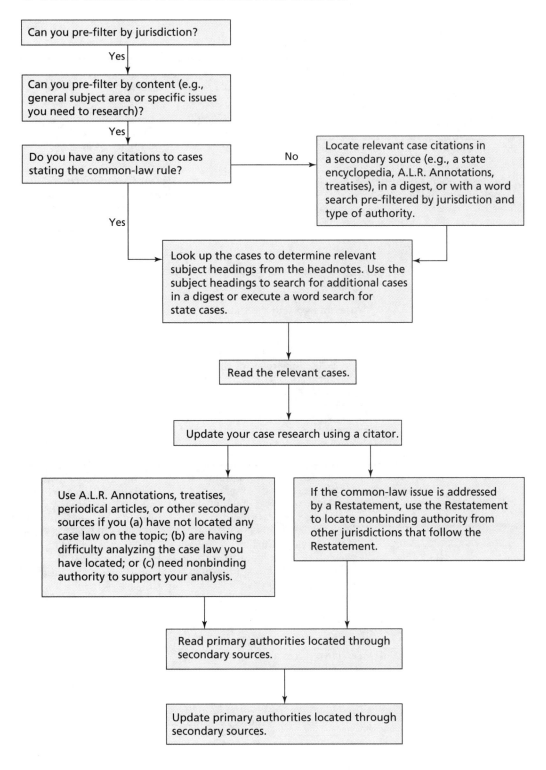

2. STATE STATUTORY RESEARCH FLOWCHART

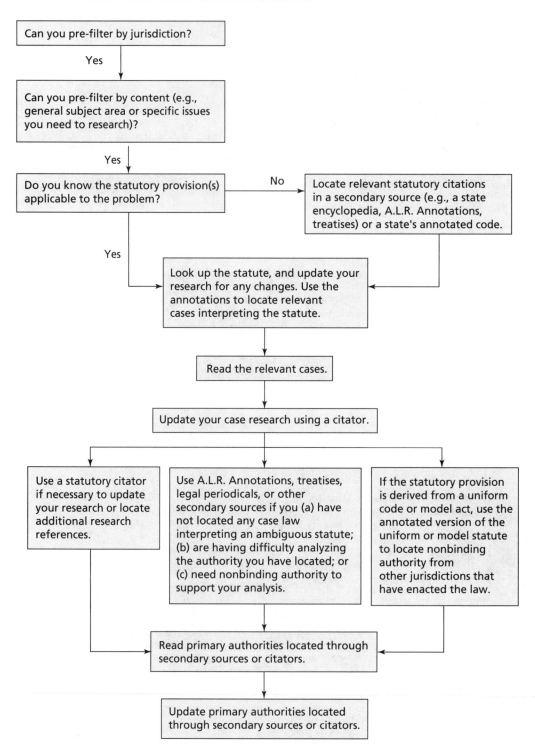

3. FEDERAL STATUTORY RESEARCH FLOWCHART

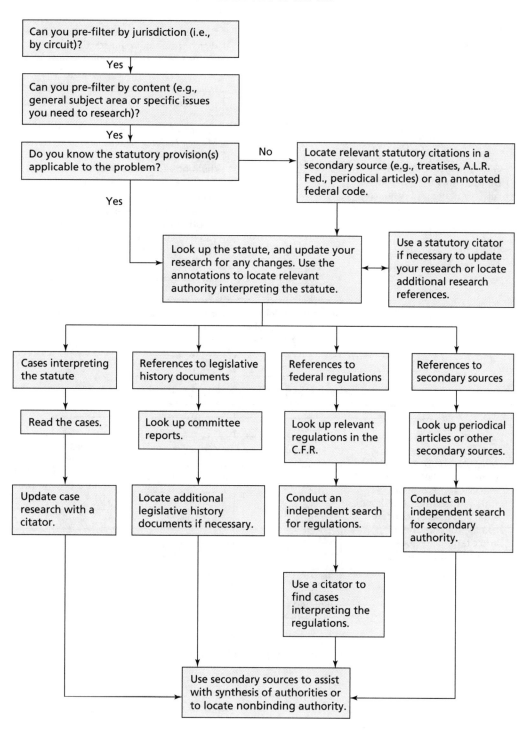

4. STATE AND FEDERAL PROCEDURAL RESEARCH FLOWCHART

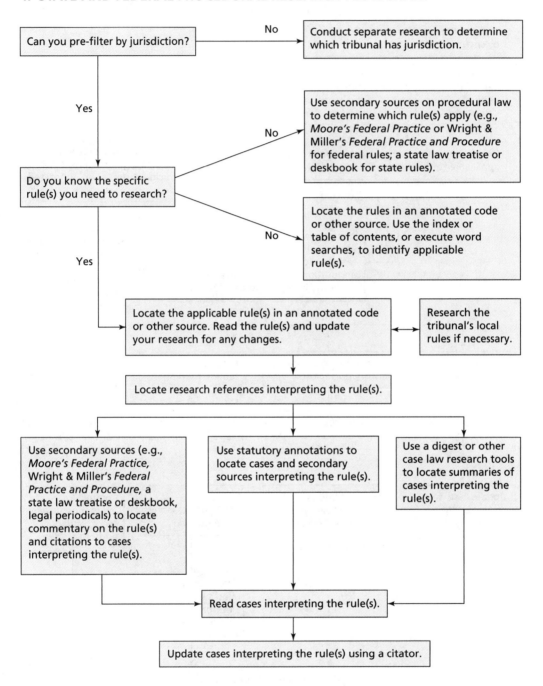

Selected Research Resources

Federal Government Websites

Congress.gov
http://congress.gov
> The Library of Congress's online source for legislative information. This site contains committee reports, the *Congressional Record*, and other legislative history documents.

govinfo.gov
https://www.govinfo.gov
> The federal government's source for many government publications, including the *Code of Federal Regulations*, the *Federal Register*, and a wide range of legislative history documents. Links to the e-CFR for updating federal regulatory research and the CyberCemetery of Former Federal Web Sites for locating archived versions of federal websites.

Library of Congress
http://www.loc.gov
> Search the online catalog of the Library of Congress and locate a wealth of legal and general information.

United States House of Representatives Office of the Law Revision Counsel
http://uscode.house.gov
> This site contains an online version of the *United States Code*.

United States Supreme Court
http://www.supremecourtus.gov
> The site for the U.S. Supreme Court.

USA.gov
http://www.usa.gov
> The U.S. government's official portal to a wide range of governmental resources.

United States Courts of Appeals
http://www.[identifier].uscourts.gov
> Each federal circuit court of appeals has its own website; insert the letters ca and the number of the circuit as the identifier in the URL above to access a numbered circuit's site, e.g., ca1 for the First Circuit, ca2 for the Second Circuit, etc. The Federal Circuit is identified as cafc, and the District of Columbia Circuit is identified as cadc.

State Government Websites

National Center for State Courts
http://www.ncsc.org
> Provides links to court websites for each state.

National Conference of State Legislatures
http://www.ncsl.org
> Provides links to legislative websites for each state.

Every state government has a portal that provides access to legal information for the state. You can locate a state's website using a search engine or through the library websites listed below.

Library Websites

Law library sites can be used to search for a wide range of legal authorities, including state and federal cases and statutes, administrative materials, secondary sources, and legal news. Those listed here are good starting points for research, but many other library sites are also useful for legal research.

Cornell Law School's Legal Information Institute
http://www.law.cornell.edu

Georgetown Law Library
http://www.ll.georgetown.edu

General Legal Research Websites

Like the law library websites, these sites provide access to a wide range of legal materials. Some can be accessed free of charge; others are fee-based services.

Free Services

All Law
http://www.alllaw.com

American Bar Association Lawlink: The Legal Research Jumpstation
http://www.americanbar.org
     Search for *lawlink jumpstation* on the ABA website.

Casetext (including CARA)
https://casetext.com

FindLaw
http://lp.findlaw.com

Hieros Gamos
http://www.hg.org

LLRX.com
http://www.llrx.com

Fee-Based Services (with free access provided to students)

Bloomberg Law
http://www.bloomberglaw.com

Lexis for law students
http://www.lexis.com/lawschool (follow the link to Lexis Advance to access full search functionality)

Ravel
http://ravellaw.com

VersusLaw
http://www.versuslaw.com

Westlaw for law students
http://lawschool.westlaw.com (follow the link to Westlaw Edge to access full search functionality)

Search Engines

General search engines can be used to locate legal information. Those listed here are specialized search engines.

DRAGNET
https://www.nyls.edu/library/library_services/dragnet1/dragnet/
     DRAGNET ("Database Retrieval Access using Google's New Electronic Technology") searches through a select group of free, law-related web sites.

Google Scholar
http://scholar.google.com
     Searches case law and scholarly literature.

Justia
https://www.justia.com/search
     Searches legal web resources.

MetaCrawler
http://www.metacrawler.com
     Allows you to execute a search through multiple search engines simultaneously.

Other Websites of Interest

ABA Journal Blawg Directory
http://www.abajournal.com/blawgs
     Contains a directory of law-related blogs.

ALWD Guide to Legal Citation
http://www.WKLegaledu.com
     Search by the author's name (Barger) or title to locate updates and information on the ALWD Guide to Legal Citation.

The Bluebook
http://www.legalbluebook.com
     Contains the online subscription version of The Bluebook, along with tips and updates available without a subscription.

Digital Commons
https://network.bepress.com
     Search or browse all content (legal and nonlegal) in the Digital Commons Network. Use the topic wheel to narrow by topic. To research a specific school's content, visit *https://www.bepress.com/categories_wdc/law-schools* and click on the link to the school.

Evernote
http://evernote.com
>   Online tool for organizing research materials.

Introduction to Basic Legal Citation
http://www.law.cornell.edu/citation
>   Provides tips on citation format.

Internet Archive Wayback Machine
https://archive.org
>   Contains archived web pages. To see what a website displayed on a
>   date in the past, enter the URL for the site, and select the date.

Martindale-Hubbell
http://www.martindale.com
>   Search for individual lawyers, firms, or government agencies
>   employing attorneys.

PowerNotes
http://powernotes.com
>   Online tool for organizing research materials.

SCOTUS Mapper
http://law.ubalt.edu/faculty/scotus-mapping/index.cfm (SCOTUS Mapping
Project, including library of maps)

https://www.courtlistener.com/visualizations/scotus-mapper (online mapping tool via Court Listener)
>   View maps tracing U.S. Supreme Court doctrines or create your
>   own map.

Social Science Research Network (SSRN)
http://www.ssrn.com
>   SSRN's Legal Scholarship Network (LSN) provides full-text access
>   to published and forthcoming legal periodical articles.

Zotero
https://www.zotero.org
>   Online tool for organizing research materials.

Subscription Services

The following subscription services may be available to you through your library's research portal.

Casemaker
> A service that provides access to a range of primary authorities.

Fastcase
> A service that provides access to a range of primary authorities. For a description of the Interactive Timeline feature, visit: *http:// www.fastcase.com/wp-content/uploads/2011/12/Part8.pdf.*

HeinOnline
> A service that provides access to legal periodicals, legislative history documents, the *Code of Federal Regulations*, and other publications.

Index to Legal Periodicals (ILP)
> A periodical index that also provides full text of selected articles.

LegalTrac
> A periodical index that also provides full text of selected articles.

ProQuest Congressional
> A service that provides access to federal legislative history documents.